Cambridge Proficiency
Examination Practice 5

Cambridge Proficiency

Examination Practice 5

University of Cambridge
Local Examinations Syndicate

CAMBRIDGE
UNIVERSITY PRESS

Published by the Press Syndicate of the University of Cambridge
The Pitt Building, Trumpington Street, Cambridge CB2 1RP
40 West 20th Street, New York, NY 10011–4211, USA
10 Stamford Road, Oakleigh, Melbourne 3166, Australia

© Cambridge University Press 1993

First published 1993

Printed in Great Britain
at the University Press, Cambridge

ISBN 0 521 44674 0 Student's Book
ISBN 0 521 44675 9 Teacher's Book
ISBN 0 521 44676 7 Set of 2 cassettes

GO

Contents

Acknowledgements

The author and publishers are grateful to the following for permission to reproduce copyright material identified in the text. It has not been possible to identify sources of all the material used and in such cases the publishers would welcome information from copyright holders.

Texts: Andre Deutsch Ltd for the extract on pp. 6–7 from *Sour Sweet*, by Timothy Mo, © Timothy Mo 1982; Faber & Faber Ltd and Alfred A. Knopf Inc. for the extract on pp. 25–6 from *Devices and Desires*, by P. D. James, © P. D. James 1989; The Economist Newspaper Ltd for the extract on p. 27, © The Economist, 26 Nov 1988; The British Museum for the extract on pp. 28–9 from their magazine, Spring 1990; Pyramid Publishers for the extract on pp. 35–6 from *Tribes* by Desmond Morris and Peter Marsh © 1988; The Independent for the extract on pp. 49–50 from *Growing old* by Anthony Sampson, and for the extract on pp. 51–2 from *A fulfilling experience that should be shared*, by David Pountney, both © The Independent 1990; Hodder & Stoughton Limited for the extract on p. 53 from *Translating (Teach Yourself)* by Ian F Finlay; Jonathan Cape Ltd and Random House Inc for the extract on pp. 61–2 from *The inner game of tennis* by Timothy Gallwey; the extract on p. 75 from *A Trinity* by William Trevor, in the *Minerva Book of Short Stories* © 1988 reprinted by permission of the Peters Fraser & Dunlop Group Ltd and Viking; the extract from *A language in common* by Marion Molteno first published by the Women's Press Ltd, 1987, 34 Great Sutton Street, London EC1V 0DX, reprinted on pp. 94–5, is used by permission of the Women's Press; the extract on pp. 101–2 from *The Driving Manual* is reproduced with the permission of the Controller of her Majesty's Stationery Office; The Independent on Sunday for the extract on pp. 104–5 from *Anyone for a holiday?* by Blake Morrison © The Independent 1990.

Photographs: p. 113 The Hulton Deutsch Collection; p. 114 (top) Popperfoto/Bob Fraser, (bottom) Popperfoto/Reuter/Will Burgess; p. 116 Popperfoto/Reuter/David Osborn; p. 117 (bottom) Popperfoto; p. 118 (left) copyright British Museum, (right) Ardea London Ltd; p. 120 Jeffrey F. Morgan; p. 121 (top) Cambridge Newspapers Ltd, (bottom) Popperfoto; p. 123 Popperfoto/AFP/Jerome Delay; p. 124 (top) Popperfoto, (bottom) Popperfoto/Reuter/George Bilyk; p. 127 (top) The Independent, (bottom) Chris Thomond; p. 130 (top and bottom) The Imperial War Museum, London.

Cartoon on p. 129 by Shaun Williams.

To the student

This book is for candidates preparing for the University of Cambridge Certificate of Proficiency in English examination and provides practice in all the written and oral papers. It contains 5 complete tests, based on the Proficiency examinations set between 1990 and 1993. The examination consists of 5 papers, as follows:

Paper 1 Reading Comprehension (1 hour)
  Section A consists of 25 multiple-choice items in the form of a sentence with a blank to be filled in by 1 of 4 words or phrases.
  Section B consists of 15 multiple-choice items based on 3 or more reading passages of different types.

Paper 2 Composition (2 hours)
  There are 5 topics from which you choose 2. The topics include discursive, descriptive and narrative essays, a directed writing exercise and an essay based on optional reading. (In these practice tests the questions based on optional reading are set on the kind of books that are prescribed each year. These are *not* the actual books prescribed for any particular year: they are just given as examples.)

Paper 3 Use of English (2 hours)
  Section A contains exercises of various kinds which test your control of English usage and grammatical structure.
  Section B consists of a passage followed by questions which test your comprehension and skill in summarising.

Paper 4 Listening Comprehension (about 30 minutes)
  You answer a variety of questions on 3 or 4 recorded passages from English broadcasts, interviews, announcements, phone messages, conversations etc. Each passage is heard twice.

Paper 5 Interview (15 to 20 minutes)
  You take part in a conversation based on a photograph, passage and other material from authentic sources linked by theme, either with a group of other candidates or with the examiner alone. The exercises in these tests include some of the type set in the examination on optional reading.

Practice Test 1

PAPER 1 READING COMPREHENSION (1 hour)

Answer all questions. Indicate your choice of answer in every case **on the separate answer sheet** *already given out, which should show your name and examination index number. Follow carefully the instructions about how to record your answers. Give* **one answer only** *to each question. Marks will not be deducted for wrong answers: your total score on this test will be the number of correct answers you give.*

SECTION A

In this section you must choose the word or phrase which best completes each sentence. **On your answer sheet** *indicate the letter A, B, C or D against the number of each item 1 to 25 for the word or phrase you choose.*

1 According to the .... of the contract, tenants must give six months' notice if they intend to leave.
   A laws   B rules   C terms   D details

2 The injured man was taken to hospital and .... for internal injuries.
   A cured   B healed   C operated   D treated

3 The door hinges had all been oiled to stop them ....
   A squeaking   B screeching   C shrieking   D squealing

4 Mary attempted to .... herself with her new boss by volunteering to take on extra work.
   A gratify   B please   C ingratiate   D commend

5 You are under no obligation .... to accept this offer.
   A indeed   B eventually   C apart   D whatsoever

6 The dealer wanted £400, I wanted to pay £300, and we finally agreed to .... the difference.
   A divide   B split   C drop   D decrease

7 I was .... in the book I was reading and didn't hear the phone.
   A distracted   B submerged   C gripped   D engrossed

8 A washing machine of this type will certainly .... up to normal domestic use.
   A hold   B stand   C come   D take

9   .... any other politician would have given way to this sort of pressure years ago.
    A Really   B Practically   C Actually   D Utterly

10 If you .... too long, you may miss a wonderful opportunity.
    A loiter   B doubt   C hover   D hesitate

11 The singer's performance was so exciting that many of his fans were .... enthusiasm.
    A carried away with   B moved to   C taken aback with
    D stirred up with

12 Passengers are .... not to leave cases and packages here.
    A commanded   B informed   C notified   D advised

13 He has an excellent .... as a criminal lawyer.
    A popularity   B fame   C regard   D reputation

14 Hardly had the van turned the corner when one of the back wheels ....
    A broke away   B turned round   C came off   D rolled down

15 There was no sound to be heard except the .... of raindrops on the roof.
    A surging   B plunging   C moistening   D pattering

16 The new teacher was .... to the needs of all the children in her care.
    A attentive   B observant   C earnest   D careful

17 He spent ten years in the army and for most of the time he was .... abroad.
    A camped   B situated   C placed   D stationed

18 Thousands of steel .... were used as the framework of the new office block.
    A girders   B beams   C piles   D stakes

19 .... efforts to combat it, drug abuse is on the increase.
    A Instead of   B In the event of   C Throughout   D Despite

20 She loved her little dog but showed surprisingly little .... when it died.
    A sentiment   B sympathy   C emotion   D involvement

21 If he tries to .... ignorance as his excuse, just tell him we've got a copy of the authorisation with his signature on it.
    A pretend   B plead   C protest   D defend

22 Would you like me to .... you another slice of chicken?
    A carve   B slash   C peel   D shave

23 Given the present economic situation, it .... be best to wait before
making further wage demands.
A seemed   B ought   C might   D should

24 The chemicals spilled over the road and left drivers .... for breath.
A suffocating   B gasping   C inhaling   D wheezing

25 The government clearly had not the slightest .... of changing the
legislation, in spite of the continued protest.
A desire   B ambition   C willingness   D intention

SECTION B

*In this section you will find after each of the passages a number of questions or
unfinished statements about the passage, each with four suggested answers or ways of
finishing. You must choose the one which you think fits best.* **On your answer sheet,
indicate the letter A, B, C or D against the number of each item 26–40 for the answer
you choose. Give one answer only** *to each question. Read each passage right through
before choosing your answers.*

FIRST PASSAGE

Urban life has always involved a balancing of opportunities and rewards
against dangers and stress; its motivating force is, in the broadest sense,
money. Opportunities to make money mean competition and competition
is stressful; it is often at its most intense in the largest cities, where
opportunities are greatest. The presence of huge numbers of people
inevitably involves more conflict, more travelling, the overloading of public
services and exposure to those deviants and criminals who are drawn to the
rich pickings of great cities. Crime has always flourished in the relative
anonymity of urban life, but today's ease of movement makes its control
more difficult than ever; there is much evidence that its extent has a direct
relationship to the size of communities. City dwellers may become trapped
in their homes by the fear of crime around them.

As a defence against these developments, city dwellers tend to use
various strategies to try and reduce the pressures upon themselves: contacts
with other people are generally made brief and impersonal; doors are kept
locked; telephone numbers may be ex-directory; journeys outside the home
are usually hurried, rather than a source of pleasure. There are other
strategies too which are positively harmful to the individual; for example,
reducing awareness through drugs or alcohol. Furthermore, all these

defensive forms of behaviour are harmful to society in general; they cause widespread loneliness and destroy the community's concern for its members. Lack of informal social contact and indifference to the misfortunes of others, if they are not personally known to oneself, are amongst the major causes of urban crime.

Inner areas of cities tend to be abandoned by the more successful and left to those who have done badly in the competitive struggle or who belong to minority groups; these people are then geographically trapped because so much economic activity has migrated to the suburbs and beyond.

Present-day architecture and planning have enormously worsened the human problems of urban life. Old-established neighbourhoods have been ruthlessly swept away, by both public and private organisations, usually to be replaced by huge, ugly, impersonal structures. People have been forced to leave their familiar homes, usually to be rehoused in tower blocks which are drab, inconvenient, and fail to provide any setting for human interaction or support. This destruction of established social structures is the worst possible approach to the difficulties of living in a town or city. Instead, every effort should be made to conserve the human scale of the environment, and to retain familiar landmarks.

26 According to the author, living in a city causes stress because there are so many people who are
A anxious to succeed.
B in need of help.
C naturally aggressive.
D likely to commit crime.

27 The author thinks that crime is increasing in cities because
A people do not communicate with their neighbours.
B criminals are difficult to trace in large populations.
C people feel anonymous there.
D the trappings of success are attractive to criminals.

28 According to the article, what is the worst problem facing people living in cities?
A crime
B finding somewhere to live
C social isolation
D drugs and alcoholism

29 The majority of people who live in inner cities do so because they
A dislike having to travel far to work.
B have been forced by circumstances to do so.
C don't like the idea of living in the suburbs.
D have turned against society.

30 Architectural changes have affected city life by
    A dispersing long-established communities.
    B giving the individual a say in planning.
    C forcing people to live on top of each other.
    D making people move to the suburbs.

31 The author's general argument is that urban life would be improved by
    A moving people out of tower blocks.
    B restoring old buildings.
    C building community centres.
    D preserving existing social systems.

SECOND PASSAGE

Lily Chen always prepared an 'evening' snack for her husband to consume on his return at 1.15a.m. This was not strictly necessary since Chen enjoyed at the unusually late hour of 11.45p.m. what the boss boasted was the best employees' dinner in any restaurant. They sat, waiters, boss, boss's mother too, at a round table and ate soup, a huge fish, vegetables, shredded pork, and a tureen of steaming rice. Lily still went ahead and prepared broth, golden-yellow with floating oily rings, and put it before her husband when he returned. She felt she would have been failing in her wifely duties otherwise. Dutifully, Chen drank the soup he raised to his mouth in the patterned porcelain spoon while Lily watched him closely from the sofa. It was far too rich for him. Lily had the gas fire burning five minutes before her husband's footfall on the stone stairs and Chen would be perspiring heavily by the time he finished, abandoning the spoon and applying the bowl to his lips to drink the last awkward inches, the beads of moisture on his forehead as salty as the broth. He fancied they fell in and over-seasoned the last of the soup. Four years ago, at the beginning of their marriage, Chen had tried leaving the last spoonful but Lily's reproachful eyes were intolerable. She was merciless now, watching him with sidelong glances from the sofa, her knees pressed closely together while she paired the baby's socks from the plastic basket on the floor. 'Did you enjoy that, Husband?' 'Was it nice?' she would enquire brightly. Chen would grunt in his stolid way, not wishing to hurt her feelings but also careful not to let himself in for a bigger bowl in the future.
    Although comfortably full, Chen would have liked a biscuit but Lily was unrelenting here as well. Sweet after salty was dangerous for the system, so she had been taught; it could upset the whole balance of the dualistic or female and male principles, yin and yang. Lily was full of incontrovertible pieces of lore like this which she had picked up from her father who had been a part-time bone-setter and Chinese boxer. For four years, therefore, Chen had been going to bed tortured with the last extremities of thirst but with his dualistic male and female principles in

harmony. This was more than could be said for Lily, Chen often thought, who concealed a steely will behind her demure exterior.

32 What was Chen's job?
   A He ran a restaurant.
   B He washed dishes.
   C He was a cook.
   D He worked as a waiter.

33 How did Chen feel about his meal at home?
   A It was too hot.
   B He looked forward to it.
   C It was well-balanced.
   D He would rather not have had it.

34 Chen always finished his soup because Lily
   A felt content if he did.
   B would then allow him a drink.
   C did not like to throw food away.
   D complained bitterly if he didn't.

35 Chen's homelife was difficult because of his wife's
   A lack of concern.
   B rigid ideas.
   C thoughtlessness.
   D unco-operative behaviour.

36 Which of the following statements correctly describes the relationship between Lily and Chen?
   A They were indifferent to each other.
   B They respected each other.
   C They made each other suffer.
   D They did not get on well.

THIRD PASSAGE

One of the greatest problems in assessing most accounts of folk customs is that they tend to give only the antiquary's point of view. After all, to most observers, the people they were looking at were simple and illiterate, unmindful of the true significance of the customs they had preserved. Why question them at length if they didn't understand the essential nature of what they were doing? So a folklorist is likely to emphasise aspects of a tradition which reflect his or her own interests or which fit in with preconceived ideas, while possibly ignoring or giving only passing mention to aspects which may, in fact, be of equal importance.

One aspect which generally gets left out of accounts is the viewpoint of the participants themselves: for instance, why they indulge in a particular activity at a particular time of year or of their lives and what feelings they experience while doing so. And now, ideas deriving from folklore studies are so widespread that they may easily have become an integral part of the attitudes of the participants in a custom. So the folklorist is rather like a man staring at a scene in a mirror who must be aware, to fully understand that scene, that his own reflection is a major part of what he is looking at.

It is, however, also true to say that many contemporary students of folklore are fully aware of the problems which beset their enquiries. Like true scientists they draw their conclusions by looking at available evidence, rather than selecting evidence which fits in with existing theories. Some have also looked away from the 'obviously' ancient and turned their attention to folklore where it thrives, in the social life of modern cities, in industry and sport etc. They may, for example, end up looking at the lore of the motor car, or of popular music, and at customs which, though they have no hints of paganism, nevertheless have much in common with older activities which do.

Many folklorists have gradually come to the conclusion that folklore is not necessarily a thing of the past, a relic of ancient and outmoded ways of thinking, but the means by which people try to make sense of the world (or to confront its lack of sense) and try to alleviate boredom and suffering.

37 Why are early accounts of folk customs unreliable?
    A The participants did not reveal the significance of their customs.
    B The participants were not aware of the meaning of their customs.
    C Folklorists did not consider the participants intelligent enough to answer the questions.
    D Folklorists undervalued the opinions of the participants.

38 Why is the study of folklore today difficult?
    A Participants insist on the accuracy of their own interpretations.
    B Participants are now influenced by earlier studies of their activities.
    C Folklorists are too concerned to justify their own theories.
    D Folklorists are often misled by unreliable earlier studies.

39 What is new about folklorists today?
    A They are now more cautious about the evidence they accept.
    B They want to investigate the more obscure areas of folklore.
    C They are studying the creation of folklore in present-day society.
    D They want to discover the links between paganism and modern social customs.

40 What does participation in folk customs mean to people?
    A It can be of psychological benefit to them.
    B It enables them to escape the problems of the modern world.
    C It can be a means of regaining ancient wisdom.
    D It is an attempt to reconstruct what is lost forever.

PAPER 2 COMPOSITION (2 hours)

*Write **two only** of the following composition exercises. Your answers must follow exactly the instructions given. Write in pen, not pencil. You are allowed to make alterations, but see that your work is clear and easy to read.*

1 Briefly describe the neighbourhood you live in and a few of the more interesting people who live and work there. (About 350 words)

2 'You are what you eat.' How important is diet to health and well-being? (About 350 words)

3 'What a strange day it had been! Losing such a small article had led to the most amazing consequences.' Use this as the first or last sentence of a story. (About 350 words)

4 Because of bad weather conditions your plane had to make an unscheduled landing.
Write a letter to the airline company complaining about the lack of food, accommodation and services provided, and demand compensation. (About 300 words)

5 Basing your answer on your reading of the prescribed text concerned, answer **one** of the following. (About 350 words)

GRAHAM GREENE: *The Quiet American*
What part does the triangular relationship between Pyle, Fowler and Phuong play in the story?

JANE AUSTEN: *Persuasion*
Explain how in *Persuasion* Anne had been forced into prudent behaviour in her youth yet was able to find romance as she grew older.

ERNEST HEMINGWAY: *A Farewell to Arms*
Would you agree that *A Farewell to Arms* is no more than the story of a love affair between an American lieutenant and an English nurse?

PAPER 3   USE OF ENGLISH   (2 hours)

SECTION A

1   *Fill each of the numbered blanks in the passage with **one** suitable word.*

Sugar was for a long time a luxury and in the opinion of the medical profession it still should be. During the nineteenth century, however, manufacturers discovered (1) .... of producing it in vast quantities and it has since become (2) .... of the staple articles of diet, particularly (3) .... the lower social classes. It has the advantages of (4) .... comparatively cheap, easily digested, rich (5) .... energy and useful for flavouring. Its major (6) .... are that it lacks every nourishing quality (7) .... that of giving energy, and (8) .... of its attractive flavour it (9) .... to displace other much more valuable foods (10) .... the diet. Most serious of all is its adverse (11) .... on health, since excessive consumption can cause heart (12) ...., obesity and dental decay. The latter is widespread among the inhabitants of western countries. From the very young to the very old, (13) .... anyone escapes. Yet if parents (14) .... drastically reduce the (15) .... of confectionery they allow (16) .... children to eat, the extent of dental decay would soon be checked. And (17) .... they were to (18) .... down their own consumption of sugar, they would suffer much (19) .... from ailments resulting directly or indirectly from their (20) .... overweight.

2 *Finish each of the following sentences in such a way that it is as similar as possible in meaning to the sentence printed before it.*

EXAMPLE: I expect that he will get there by lunchtime.

ANSWER: I expect him *to get there by lunchtime.*

   a) The rail workers do not intend to call off their strike.

       The rail workers have no ....

   b) Mrs Scott is proud of her cooking.

       Mrs Scott prides ....

   c) It was the goalkeeper who saved the match for us.

       If it hadn't ....

   d) I wasn't a bit surprised to hear that Karen had changed her job.

       It came ....

   e) You can try to get Tim to lend you his car but you won't succeed.

       There's no point ....

   f) John didn't celebrate until he received the offer of promotion in writing.

       Not until ....

   g) I don't really like her, even though I admire her achievements.

       Much ....

   h) It's thought that the accident was caused by human error.

       The accident is ....

3 *Fill each of the blanks with a suitable word or phrase.*

   EXAMPLE: He doesn't mind one way or the other; it makes *no difference to* him.

   a) You are not the first person .... by that dog.

   b) David refused to co-operate, no .... we begged him to.

   c) So it was you? I might .... involved somehow.

d) We'd better wait a few more minutes .... anyone else arrives.

e) Even if I .... to the party, I wouldn't have wanted to go.

f) It's high time they .... they'll be coming or not.

4 *For each of the sentences below, write a new sentence* as similar as possible in meaning to the original sentence *but using the word given. This word* must not be altered *in any way.*

EXAMPLE: Not many people attended the meeting.
turnout

ANSWER: *There was a poor turnout for the meeting.*

a) Some people say that Tsiolkovsky invented the space rocket.
credited

....

b) I daren't turn on the television because the baby might wake up.
fear

....

c) Some people will do anything to lose weight.
lengths

....

d) The two theories appear to be completely different.
common

....

e) Several members of the committee said they were worried about the chairman's proposals.
concern

....

f) The river Volta overflowed last year.
burst

....

13

g) He doesn't appreciate his wife.
   granted

   ....

h) The number of people out of work has been going down little by little.
   gradual

   ....

SECTION B

5 *Read the following passage, then answer the questions which follow it.*

Travel Writing

Within the last few years a spate of travel books has flooded into the
bookshops, and the overwhelming majority have not been worth
publishing.

They are packaged for the general reader, but are usually of interest
only to the specialist. I find that any competent writer can produce a   5
worthwhile book for those interested in specific areas. Thus, if someone
frequently takes a holiday in Aleppo, he may be gripped by the
controversy over whether a certain mosque was built with local or
imported mud. But it is rare to find the travel writer who can make this
controversy interesting to the general reader.   10

The true difficulty of writing a first-rate travel book for the non-
specialist can be proved by the numerous failures when publishers have
sent away their best authors to write about their travels. Even prize-
winning writers have failed to pull it off. Indeed the indefinable
ingredients for a memorable travel book are so rare that a surprising   15
number of writers have not been able to repeat their one success, even
though they keep on trying. This success is often their first travel book
and the reader usually senses within a few pages that it has been
touched with magic. I use the word 'magic' because there is rarely a
logical reason why the author's subsequent attempts are nowhere near   20
so good. When I have delicately discussed this subject with authors,
they have sometimes described their one magical book as 'having
almost written itself'.

Because it is remarkably hard to write entertainingly about travel, a
number of writers relate grotesque lies in order to keep the reader's   25
attention. This has always been the case. South American travel books
traditionally include a scene where a canoeist is torn to pieces by
piranha fish; yet despite extensive research among my acquaintances,

14

some of whom have spent weeks wading in South American rivers, I have never heard of one authentic account. 30

Do these lies matter, considering that so many travel writers seem to indulge in them? Having waded through hundreds of books, I have decided that there are two very different types of lie. There is the piranha-type, which is devised in order to pander to what the public wants, and frequently to boost the macho image of the author. This is 35 totally unacceptable. Furthermore it is often boring, because we end up by not believing even the true bits. It is also immoral, because the printed word is to some extent holy – a record which people will read in later decades, often accepting it as true.

Some authors tell lies in an effort to get closer to the truth. This is 40 hard to explain or defend, but I have reluctantly come to accept it. It is their way of getting at the 'larger truth' through a distortion of existing facts. Every author has to some extent done this by reducing time. No-one would ploddingly describe the boring stages of the journey at the same length as the exciting ones. 45

As it is so difficult to select the best reading from the torrent, I discriminate increasingly in favour of those authors who speak the local language. If the author cannot communicate, there is little chance of any real insight into a foreign country. Before Colin Thubron went to China he learnt the language, and *Behind the Wall* would have been nowhere 50 near so good if he hadn't.

Worthwhile insights can also be guaranteed from those authors who have actually lived in a country.

Several of our most celebrated travel writers have been unlucky enough to be born without the humanity or soul to form a relationship 55 with a country or its people. They can never get right under its skin, even though they are spellbindingly clever at writing. Their books make elegant and entertaining reading today, but in a few decades will be forgotten.

a) Explain the phrase 'gripped by the controversy'. (lines 7–8)

....

....

b) What is meant by the sentence 'Even prize-winning writers have failed to pull it off'? (lines 13–14)

....

....

c) What is meant by the words 'touched with magic'? (line 19)

....

....

d) What subject has the writer of the passage discussed with authors?

....

....

e) Why does the author mention piranha fish?

....

....

....

f) Explain what the author finds 'immoral' (line 37) and why.

....

....

....

g) What 'distortion of existing facts' does the author find acceptable?
(lines 42–43)

....

....

h) What is the 'torrent' referred to in line 46?
Which two words in the first paragraph are echoed by the word
'torrent'? (line 46)

....

....

....

i) According to the passage, what is *Behind the Wall* an example of, and why?

....

....

j) Explain what the author means by saying 'They can never get right under its skin.' (line 56)

....

....

k) How does the writer of the passage account for the present popularity of some books which he feels will soon be forgotten?

....

l) In a paragraph of 60–80 words, explain what qualities the author thinks make a good travel book.

....

....

....

....

....

....

....

....

....

....

....

PAPER 4   LISTENING COMPREHENSION
(about 30 minutes)

PART ONE

*You will hear a recorded message giving details about what is on at theatres in London. Look at the notepad on your question paper. For questions **1–8** listen particularly to the information about **The Great Mogul** show and **The Little Pony** on **Thursdays**, and fill in the missing information in the gaps in the notepad.*

Theatre – Thursday

	The Great Mogul	The Little Pony
Theatre?	1	5
Time (s)	2	6
Price	3	Children £2.40 (double ticket) Adults £4.80 (double ticket)
Suitable for what age?	Any	7
Tel:	4	8

PART TWO

*You will hear an interview with a professional dancer called Keely Garfield. For questions **9–14** indicate the correct answer by putting a tick in the box next to the appropriate letter.*

9   Why is the reporter surprised at the activity of the old people?

A They are doing very vigorous exercises.	A
B It is an extremely hot day.	B
C Their tutor is very young.	C
D They are very happy.	D

10   What are the exercises designed mainly to promote?

A strength	A
B speed	B
C flexibility	C
D stamina	D

11   Which exercises can the old lady do?

A leg and arm exercises only	A
B only three exercises	B
C all the exercises	C
D neck, head and tummy exercises	D

12   How did Keely get the old man to join in?

A by being kind and sympathetic	A
B by letting him sit down	B
C by expressing her irritation with him	C
D by persuading him to use his arms	D

13   Why does Keely do this unpaid work?

A She can't get enough paid work.

B It helps to keep her fit.

C She finds it very amusing.

D She likes helping her students.

A	
B	
C	
D	

14   How did Keely know she had got through to her withdrawn pupil?

A He started to do exercises.

B He took her hand.

C He kissed her.

D He made everyone laugh.

A	
B	
C	
D	

PART THREE

You will hear an interview with an astronomer about a newly discovered planet. For questions **15–20**, *fill in the missing information in the spaces provided.*

Name of Planet		15
Size (compared with Jupiter)		16
Discovery announced by	National Science Foundation	
Colour of companion star		17
Distance of Star from Earth		18
How bright was the planet?		19
Kit Peak Observatory sited in		20

PART FOUR

You will hear a discussion about maintaining aircraft. For questions **21–24** *indicate the correct answer by putting a tick in the box next to the appropriate letter.*

21   Why will the floor of the aircraft be taken out?

A to examine the metal in the aircraft

B to check the systems beneath the floor

C to refurbish the cabin and galleys

D to inspect the seat mountings

A	
B	
C	
D	

22   Why don't small airlines always use the maintenance facilities provided by large airlines?

A Big airlines charge too much money.

B Big airlines find the maintenance too expensive.

C Companies like ATEL offer better maintenance facilities.

D Companies like ATEL offer total maintenance support.

A	
B	
C	
D	

23   Why does most corrosion occur under the galley and toilet areas?

A Liquid gets spilled in the galleys.

B Corrosive liquids are used as antifreeze.

C The toilets overflow when blocked.

D Water escapes from the pipes.

A	
B	
C	
D	

24   Why is corrosion beneath the toilet and galley areas NOT dangerous?

A The corrosion does NOT affect major structure.

B The corrosion is seldom extensive.

C ATEL treat the affected areas in time.

D There is sufficient metal for safety.

A	
B	
C	
D	

PAPER 5 INTERVIEW (15–20 minutes)

You will be asked to take part in a conversation with a group of other students or with your teacher. The conversation will be based on one particular topic area or theme, for example holidays, work, food.

Of course each interview will be different for each student or group of students, but a *typical* interview is described below.

★ At the start of the interview you will be asked to talk about one of the photographs among the Interview Exercises at the back of the book.

★ You will then be asked to discuss one of the passages at the back of the book. Your teacher may ask you to talk about its content, where you think it comes from, who the author or speaker is, whether you agree or disagree with it, and so on. You will *not* be asked to read the passage aloud, but you may quote parts of it to make your point.

★ You may then be asked to discuss for example an advertisement, a leaflet, extract from a newspaper etc. Your teacher will tell you which of the Interview Exercises to look at.

★ You may also be asked to take part in an activity with a group of other students or your teacher. Your teacher will tell you which section among the Interview Exercises you should look at.

Practice Test 2

PAPER 1   READING COMPREHENSION   (1 hour)

Answer all questions. Indicate your choice of answer in every case **on the separate answer sheet** *already given out, which should show your name and examination index number. Follow carefully the instructions about how to record your answers. Give* **one answer only** *to each question. Marks will not be deducted for wrong answers: your total score on this test will be the number of correct answers you give.*

SECTION A

In this section you must choose the word or phrase which best completes each sentence. **On your answer sheet** *indicate the letter A, B, C or D against the number of each item 1 to 25 for the word or phrase you choose.*

1   In spite of his poor education, he was a most .... speaker.
   A articulate   B ambiguous   C attentive   D authoritarian

2   Wasn't it you yourself .... the door open?
   A to leave   B to have left   C who left   D that should leave

3   You should .... at least three days for the journey.
   A expect   B permit   C accept   D allow

4   .... of the financial crisis, all they could do was hold on and hope that things would improve.
   A At the bottom   B At the height   C On the top   D In the end

5   Could you possibly .... me at the next committee meeting?
   A stand in for   B make up for   C fall back on   D keep in with

6   It is regretted that there can be no .... to this rule.
   A exclusion   B alternative   C exception   D deviation

7   Complete the form as .... in the notes below.
   A insisted   B specified   C implied   D devised

8   If only motorists .... drive more carefully!
   A might   B shall   C would   D should

9 I've only met Stephen in a social context – he's an unknown .... where work's concerned.
   A quantity   B option   C type   D category

10 She tried to set .... a few minutes each day for her exercises.
   A about   B down   C aside   D in

11 People convicted of murder in Britain are no longer .... to death.
   A sent   B punished   C judged   D sentenced

12 Such relaxed days were few and far .... in her hectic life.
   A off   B out   C beyond   D between

13 He was deaf to everything .... than what he wanted to hear.
   A other   B apart   C else   D except

14 The fact that trade links were well developed at this time .... some plausibility to his opinion.
   A provides   B supplies   C lends   D offers

15 He always .... this town with his cousin.
   A associates   B reminds   C relates   D reminisces

16 It is very important to check the .... print in any contract.
   A little   B tiny   C small   D minute

17 A(n) .... has been ordered into why so many safety rules were broken just before the accident occurred.
   A inquiry   B research   C search   D query

18 I am afraid that you will be .... responsible if anything goes wrong.
   A taken   B held   C carried   D brought

19 She saw .... the deception immediately.
   A round   B past   C into   D through

20 The young men were .... guilty of shoplifting.
   A found   B convicted   C accused   D condemned

21 We are prepared to overlook the error on this occasion .... your previous good work.
   A in the light of   B thanks to   C with a view to   D with regard to

22 The shop assistant said he would check to see if he had any more copies of the book in ....
   A surplus   B supply   C stock   D store

23 When I got my case back, it had been damaged .... repair.
    A above   B beyond   C over   D further

24 The woman's clothes gave no .... to her origin.
    A sign   B signal   C clue   D hint

25 In his absence, I would like to thank all concerned on my brother's ....
    A behalf   B part   C business   D interest

SECTION B

*In this section you will find after each of the passages a number of questions or
unfinished statements about the passage, each with four suggested answers or ways of
finishing. You must choose the one which you think fits best.* **On your answer sheet,
indicate the letter A, B, C or D against the number of each item** **26–40** *for the answer
you choose. Give* **one answer only** *to each question. Read each passage right through
before choosing your answers.*

FIRST PASSAGE

Jonathan Reeves's parents had moved from their small terraced house in
south London to a flat in a modern block overlooking the sea just outside
Cromer. Sometimes it seemed that their thick-pile wool and nylon carpets
had absorbed and deadened not only their footsteps. His mother's calm
response to any event was either 'Very nice', equally appropriate to an
enjoyable dinner, a royal engagement or birth, or a spectacular sunrise, or
'Terrible, terrible, isn't it? You wonder sometimes what the world's coming
to', which covered events as diverse as Kennedy's assassination, a particularly gruesome murder, or a terrorist bomb. But she didn't wonder what the
world was coming to. Wonder was an emotion long since stifled by deep
Axminster carpets, mohair, underfelt. It seemed to Jonathan that they lived
together in amity because their emotions, debilitated by under-use or
undernourishment, couldn't cope with anything as robust as a row. At the
first sign of it his mother would say 'Don't raise your voice, dear, I don't like
rows.' Disagreement, never intense, was expressed in peevish resentment
which died through lack of energy to keep it going.

To her acquaintances and to those she might have called friends, his
mother would always speak of her husband as Mr Reeves. 'Mr Reeves is
very highly thought of by Mr Wainwright.' 'Of course, you could say that
Mr Reeves IS the carpet department of Hobbs and Wainwright.' The store
represented those aspirations, traditions and orthodoxies that others found
in their profession, in their school, regiment or religion. Mr Wainwright
senior was headmaster, colonel, their high priest; their occasional Sunday
attendances at the local church merely a gesture to a lesser God. And they

25

were never regular worshippers. Jonathan suspected that this was deliber-
ate. People might want to get to know them, involve them in mothers'
meetings, Sunday-school outings, might even want to visit. On the Friday
of his first week at secondary school, the form bully had said 'Reeves's dad
is a shop assistant at Hobbs and Wainwright. He sold my mum a rug last
week,' and had minced across the room, hands obsequiously clasped. 'I
know madam will find that mixture extremely hardwearing. It's a very
popular line.' The laughter had been sycophantic but uneasy and the
teasing, for lack of popular support, had quickly died. Most of their fathers
had even less prestigious jobs.

26 The way Jonathan's mother reacted to happy events shows that she
   A was emotionally self-disciplined.
   B had an unsympathetic character.
   C did not really enjoy them.
   D did not discriminate between them.

27 The family lived together peacefully because they
   A disliked arguments.
   B lacked strong emotions.
   C seldom disagreed.
   D hardly ever spoke to each other.

28 The most important institution in Mr Reeves's life was
   A the church.
   B school.
   C work.
   D the army.

29 Why did Jonathan's parents not attend the local church regularly?
   A They were unsociable.
   B They disapproved of the services.
   C They felt unwelcome.
   D They disliked going out.

30 The form bully tried to show that Jonathan's father was
   A weak.
   B socially inferior.
   C poorly educated.
   D dishonest.

SECOND PASSAGE

A Victorian idea is back in favour: many poor people are better off when they are pulled back into the labour market. The idea was first revived in the United States. There, in its harshest form, the unemployed work in exchange for welfare. But countries with governments to the left of America's, including Australia and France, are now also exploiting ways to link income support and employment policy.

For people on the political right, it seems deplorable to encourage the poor to rely on the state for cash, because they get hooked on government help and accustomed to being poor. For those on the left, it seems deplorable to allow workers to drop out of the job market for long periods, because it makes it harder for them to find new jobs. For both, the answer is to get the poor to work.

Most industrial countries have a two-tier system of social protection: a social-security scheme, where workers and their bosses make regular contributions in exchange for payments to workers when they are unemployed, sick or retired; and a safety-net, to give some income to those poor people who have exhausted their social insurance or who have none. The former is usually not means tested but, for the unemployed, is of limited duration; the latter is almost always tied to income. The public tend to approve of contributory benefits. Safety-net benefits are less popular. Yet they have grown more rapidly. An increasing proportion of the poor are people for whom the contributory systems were never designed: the young, and lone mothers. In consequence, payments which carry a clear entitlement have become less significant, compared with those which appear to depend purely on state charity.

The rise in the bill for the unpopular kind of social protection comes at a time when governments want to curb state spending. It comes, too, at a time when many countries have done almost everything they can think of to protect the poor. A decade ago many on the left argued that poverty was usually caused by circumstances outside the control of the poor – a lack of jobs, disability, old age, racial discrimination, broken marriages. One way or another, governments have tried to tackle most of these problems. Still the poor remain.

31 The United States was the first country in modern times to
    A investigate ways of exploiting the talents of poor people.
    B stop paying benefit to the unemployed.
    C insist that recipients had to work to receive benefit.
    D ignore the suffering of the unemployed.

32 A safety-net benefit system is one
    A based on the recipient's prior contributions.
    B of limited duration.
    C that depends on state charity.
    D that pays according to the claimant's social insurance.

33 If you become unemployed, you are likely to receive a payment
   A based on your previous earnings.
   B based on an assessment of your means.
   C for as long as it takes to find another job.
   D related to your previous contributions.

34 The general attitude of the public towards benefits is that
   A young people and lone mothers should receive them.
   B entitlement should depend on contributions.
   C charity should be a matter for the state.
   D safety-net benefits are too expensive.

35 Existing social security systems are increasingly expensive to operate
    because
   A more people have lost their jobs.
   B many countries have done all they can for the poor.
   C poverty has increased uncontrollably.
   D more people are in the safety-net category.

THIRD PASSAGE

The outcome of deceit and the proof of gullibility, fakes are among the least
loved and most elusive products of the market in relics of the past. Maker
and buyer are generally united in a conspiracy of silence, the one to escape
the penalties of wrong doing, the other to preserve his own reputation, and
that of the market as a whole. Occasionally fakes are caught in a brief blaze
of infamy, but even then they generally disappear, hastily disposed of by
the collector, dealer or curator caught in possession. For this reason it tends
to be the museums and galleries that do not practise disposal which have
the best collections of fakes.

    The general invisibility of fakes is regrettable, for, if immoral and
embarrassing, fakes are also entertaining and informative. The product of
endlessly varied ingenuity, they reach the heights of imagination and
technical virtuosity as well as the depths of deceit. It is their very
deceptiveness which makes fakes more than merely entertaining. Artists or
craftsmen who copy the work of the past inevitably put something of
themselves into the copy, because they see what they are copying with the
eyes of their time. But they may also, quite deliberately, introduce varia-
tions of the given theme which accord with their own creative impulse.
Fakes, by their nature, demand the sacrifice of individualism. Successful
fakers have, so far as possible, to think themselves into the persona of the
original maker. So their work is the most accurate possible representation of
their view of the past and, if successful, of the view of those who are taken
in by it. Any distortions that later become apparent represent in essential
form the shift in perception between their day and ours.

A second advantage of fakes, particularly of art and antiques, is that they tend to be the product of pure greed, untainted by the quirks of individual creativity. As such they respond to the demands of the market more accurately, quickly and sensitively than the works of a creative artist. The successful fake represents exactly what collectors wanted, so well in fact that many fakes have enjoyed more popular success than the real thing – they are in a sense the perfect illustrations to a history of taste.

Thirdly, fakes, by their nature, are produced and marketed in a climate of luxury. Both maker and dealer work to ensure that their products pass every obvious test. And so fakes provide an excellent guide to what each generation regarded as the essential hallmarks of authenticity – one seeks unblemished perfection, the next may be convinced by extensive signs of wear and tear, while the next again may be more concerned with documentary provenance or scientific tests than with close examination of the object itself.

But fakes are more than material evidence for the study of changing attitudes. They are also deeply subversive objects which raise difficult questions about conflicting notions of authenticity, the reality of our relationship with the past and the reliability of aesthetic judgements.

36   According to the passage, who is most likely to retain a fake once it has been discovered?
     A   an art dealer
     B   a museum curator
     C   a private collector
     D   a creative artist

37   Why is the discovery of fakes embarrassing?
     A   The public has been given false information.
     B   Fakes provide examples of faulty workmanship.
     C   Fakes demonstrate that someone's judgement has been poor.
     D   A lot of money has been paid for an item that is not genuine.

38   What makes a fake informative?
     A   It shows the assumptions current at a particular time.
     B   It provides an example of creativity and ingenuity.
     C   It demonstrates the skills of the faker.
     D   It shows how the original artist worked.

39   According to the article, what is the usual reason for the creation of fakes?
     A   to fill a gap in the market
     B   to deceive the experts
     C   to make as much money as possible
     D   to prove it can be done

40 How have fakes reflected changing attitudes over the years?
    A Different types of objects have been faked at different times.
    B People's views about what is authentic have varied.
    C People have accepted different amounts of documentation.
    D Some generations have been more critical than others.

PAPER 2 COMPOSITION (2 hours)

*Write **two only** of the following composition exercises. Your answers must follow exactly the instructions given. Write in pen, not pencil. You are allowed to make alterations, but see that your work is clear and easy to read.*

1 Describe some of the events in your childhood that have made a lasting impression on you. (About 350 words)

2 'Private cars are no longer the most efficient or desirable form of transport.' Discuss this statement. (About 350 words)

3 Write a short story ending with the words: 'He had, after all, survived. He now had a future to look forward to.' (About 350 words)

4 The following are points from a film review which you have read in an arts magazine. Having seen the film yourself, you disagree with what was written. Write a letter to the Editor of the magazine expressing your point of view. (About 300 words)

> – A film of poor quality – story very difficult to understand – acting of low standard – far too long – worth seeing only because of the excellent special effects.

5 Basing your answer on your reading of the prescribed text concerned, answer **one** of the following. (About 350 words)

ERNEST HEMINGWAY: *A Farewell to Arms*
The book has been described as an anti-war novel. Describe some of the incidents in the book which might support this judgement.

OSCAR WILDE: *The Importance of Being Earnest*
What is 'Bunburying' and how does it contribute to the development of the plot?

RUTH RENDELL: *A Judgement in Stone*
Comment on the ways various members of the Coverdale family relate to Eunice.

PAPER 3   USE OF ENGLISH   (2 hours)

SECTION A

1   *Fill each of the numbered blanks in the passage with* **one** *suitable word.*

The use of audio-description – a technique designed to enable blind people to enjoy the theatre – was pioneered in America in 1981. While continuing to listen in the (1) .... way to stage dialogue and sound, visually-impaired (2) .... of the audience also receive a commentary on what is (3) .... seen.

For (4) .... who reluctantly give up the theatre when they begin to lose their (5) ...., audio-description can revive a valued interest. For those, however, who have always enjoyed the theatre (6) .... total blindness, audio-description presents a whole new dimension.

It is not (7) .... to see the lights go down to be caught up in (8) .... sense of anticipation which gradually silences and unites the audience. (9) .... the curtain has gone up, it is simply a case of total concentration (10) .... as not to miss one word, tone, nuance or stage sound that (11) .... provide a clue (12) .... some visual happening. Even (13) .... sight, theatre can be a delight, but there are innumerable gaps to be filled. Audio-description is the (14) .... solution. It (15) .... you in the picture by providing explanatory comments before the curtain goes up, and then audio commentary is relayed (16) .... an earphone by a person (17) .... is standing at the side or back of the stage (18) .... the performance.

Obviously (19) .... can replace lost sight but to a wonderful and perhaps surprising (20) .... audio-description makes it possible to *see* a play without sight. It is an exciting glimpse of things to come.

2 *Finish each of the following sentences in such a way that it is as similar as possible in meaning to the sentence printed before it.*

EXAMPLE: I expect that he will get there by lunchtime.

ANSWER: I expect him *to get there by lunchtime.*

a) House prices have risen dramatically this year.

There has ....

b) This affair does not concern you.

This affair is no ....

c) You must submit articles for the magazine by June 18th.

The final date ....

d) Although Christopher was the stronger of the two, his attacker soon overpowered him.

Despite his ....

e) What a surprise to see you here!

Fancy ....

f) I don't intend to apologise to either of them.

I have ....

g) It was only when I left home that I realised how much my father meant to me.

Not until ....

h) The only reason the party was a success was that a famous film star attended.

Had it not ....

3   *Fill each of the blanks with a suitable word or phrase.*

EXAMPLE: He doesn't mind one way or the other; it makes *no difference to* him.

a)   He found your remarks offensive. You really .... to him like that.

b)   They soon realised .... simpler the new system was.

c)   .... good trying to ring Julia. She's gone away for the weekend.

d)   Even if Richard had arrived on time it's doubtful .... somewhere to park his car.

e)   That .... James you saw at the cinema yesterday. He's on holiday abroad.

f)   I didn't want to ring the doorbell .... asleep.

4   *For each of the sentences below, write a new sentence* **as similar as possible in meaning to the original sentence** *but using the word given. This word* **must not be altered** *in any way.*

EXAMPLE: Not many people attended the meeting.
          turnout

ANSWER: *There was a poor turnout for the meeting.*

a)   Gerald never had enough to live on until he married that rich businesswoman.
     short

     ....

b)   William decided that an actor's life was not for him.
     cut

     ....

c)   The President arranged for me to use his chauffeur-driven car whenever I liked.
     disposal

     ....

d) My cat has lost its appetite.
off

....

e) The children made every effort to please their father.
best

....

f) His behaviour was rather a shock to me.
aback

....

g) They decided not to go by boat because they thought they would be seasick.
fear

....

h) The bank robbers escaped in a stolen car.
getaway

....

SECTION B

5 *Read the following passage, then answer the questions which follow it.*

Tribal Behaviour

Man is a tribal animal. To ignore it or deny it – as so many priests and politicians do – is to court disaster. The tribal qualities of the human species colour almost every aspect of our social lives. If we were ever to lose them, it would mean that we had mutated into another species altogether.   5

The word 'tribe' conjures up images of 'primitive' societies, near-naked warriors and mystical ceremonies. Tribalism, to most of us, represents an earlier stage in the evolution of the human race – something which came to an end with the advent of 'civilisation'. Yet tribalism has never disappeared. Because we are essentially social   10
animals, we have a drive to establish particular forms of affiliation with other people. Identification with others of our own nationality is not in

itself enough: it is too abstract, it lacks the sense of true bonding which can be established only in the context of smaller groups.

The modern relics of ancient tribalism are everywhere around us: in our committees, our juries, our teams and our squads: in our councils, our governments, our board members, our clubs: in our secret societies, our protest groups, our childhood gangs.

As our national units become increasingly large, so we create social units on a more human scale. Even in the anonymous spread of our major cities, people band together to create modern tribes which share the basic features of traditional ones.

Tribal feelings can be used constructively or destructively. Given half a chance they will be employed to good effect, but if the tribal urges of a particular group are frustrated they are likely to find an alternative and often damaging outlet. They cannot be suppressed because they are too basic. If the ruling authorities in any society deny the expression of tribalism, the young males will not simply remain calm and passive. Instead, they will form unofficial tribes and attack the culture which has attempted to cut them off from their primeval inheritance.

This process can be seen at work whenever gangs of alienated young males gather. They form gangs of muggers, thugs and hooligans, and then express all their pent-up tribal feelings against the police, the military or any other manifestation of conformist authority.

The excitement is the same – the planning and the tactics, the strategies and the schemes, the risks and skin-tingling dangers, the escapades and the endless story-telling about those escapades. The whole tribal scene is recreated out of the chaos of their oppressed lives.

The same age-old urge lies behind tribal games, whether the groups concerned are establishment-backed or rebels: cricketers or football hooligans, commandos or criminals, trades unionists or terrorists. All obey basically the same tribal rules.

Without the adventurous risk-taking, active co-operation and organisational restraint that operates within each of these groups, we would not have been able to build our civilisations. On the other hand, we would also have avoided war and all the other forms of aggressive disruption, from the most savage forms of terrorism to the mildest of group protests.

But we can never live without it as long as we remain human. So it is better that we learn to live with this amazing potential that has, in a mere 10,000 years, carried us from the Stone Age to the Space Age. Learning to live with it implies learning to recognise it in all its manifestations.

a) In your own words explain why priests and politicians should recognise that man is 'a tribal animal'. (line 1)

....

....

b) Using your own words, say what the result of losing our 'tribal qualities' would be. (line 2)

....

....

c) What assumption underlies the attitudes of 'civilised' societies towards tribalism?

....

....

d) Why is 'identification with others of our own nationality' considered to be inadequate? (line 12)

....

....

....

e) What is the connection between governments and major cities? Which two phrases underline this connection?

....

....

....

f) According to the writer why can't 'tribal urges' always be kept in check? (line 24)

....

g) In what sense might a tribe be described as 'unofficial'? (line 29)

....

....

....

h) What two reasons does the writer offer for the behaviour of hooligans?

....

....

....

i) What assumption does the writer make about the lives of muggers, thugs and hooligans?

....

j) The writer suggests that there are positive and negative sides to group behaviour. Give **one** example of **each**.

....

....

k) To what does the phrase 'this amazing potential' refer? (line 50)

....

l) In a paragraph of 60–80 words, explain how, in the opinion of the author, today's societies illustrate tribal rules.

....

....

....

....

....

....

....

....

....

....

....

....

....

PAPER 4   LISTENING COMPREHENSION
(about 30 minutes)

PART ONE

You will hear a man talking about his educational experiences. For questions **1–4**
indicate the correct answer by putting a tick in the box next to the appropriate letter.

1   Why did the speaker not go to university?

    A The courses were inappropriate.

    B His headmaster advised against it.

    C He disliked traditional establishments.

    D His parents could not afford it.

A	
B	
C	
D	

2   The speaker considers his parents were

    A encouraging.

    B hostile.

    C understanding.

    D indifferent.

A	
B	
C	
D	

3   He felt disappointed because the headmaster

    A would not listen to him.

    B did not impress his father.

    C gave him an unfair report.

    D failed to understand him.

A	
B	
C	
D	

4   The speaker feels that people who have a degree from university

A are at an unfair advantage when looking for a job.

B have more relevant experience for a job in the media.

C are at no particular advantage when looking for a job.

D have no relevant experience for a job in the media.

A	
B	
C	
D	

PART TWO

You will hear part of a discussion programme in which an astrologer is being interviewed. For questions 5–9 indicate the correct answer by putting a tick in the box next to the appropriate letter.

5   Why did Margery take an interest in astrology?

A She felt naturally attracted to it.

B She was asked to do some research.

C She had retired from television.

D She was unhappy with her life.

A	
B	
C	
D	

6   How did Margery feel when she had her chart read?

A confused

B sceptical

C surprised

D shocked

A	
B	
C	
D	

7   Margery says that astrologers

A have strong beliefs.

B are very artistic.

C are keen astronomers.

D practise a religion.

A	
B	
C	
D	

8   Margery thinks that astrology has helped her to

   A evaluate her own situation.

   B predict her own future.

   C make decisions about her career.

   D avoid possible problems.

A	
B	
C	
D	

9   When dealing with public figures and events, astrologers can be accused of

   A misinterpreting history.

   B being secretive.

   C being inaccurate.

   D stating the obvious.

A	
B	
C	
D	

PART THREE

You will hear part of a public meeting held to discuss plans for a new town. For questions **10–19**, *indicate whether you think each statement is* TRUE *or* FALSE *by putting a tick in the appropriate box.*

	True	False
10 The meeting will decide which team will develop the area.		
11 The first objector suggests the meeting is a waste of time.		
12 The plan to develop the new town has already been approved.		
13 The country needs to find new areas for industry.		
14 The local cities can no longer accommodate industrial workers.		
15 Mrs West is against the idea of new towns in general.		
16 Mr Lester finds Metcalf an unattractive village.		
17 Mrs Thomas is worried about Metcalf becoming a tourist attraction.		
18 Mr Lester will ensure that adequate medical services are provided.		
19 Mr Lester persuades the meeting that the development is a good idea.		

PART FOUR

Listen to Melanie talking about the work she has had done on her new house. For questions **20–24** *indicate the correct answer by putting a tick in the box next to the appropriate letter.*

20   What did the builders come to do on Tuesday morning?

A give advice about the walls

B remove old plaster from the walls

C repair a crack in the walls

D re-plaster the walls

A	
B	
C	
D	

21   Who caused the flood in the kitchen?

A the speaker herself

B a neighbour

C one of the builders

D the speaker didn't know

A	
B	
C	
D	

22   How was the mess cleared up?

A with towels and newspapers

B with the speaker's bathtowel

C with paper towels

D with paper and kitchen cloths

A	
B	
C	
D	

23   The speaker took the morning off work because

A she wanted to be there at the outset.

B the water pipe was damaged.

C the builders wanted her to be there.

D she wanted to help the builders clear up.

A	
B	
C	
D	

24 The preparations for Melanie's friend's visit were

    A relaxed.

    B routine.

    C hurried.

    D disastrous.

A	
B	
C	
D	

PAPER 5   INTERVIEW   (15–20 minutes)

You will be asked to take part in a conversation with a group of other students or with your teacher. The conversation will be based on one particular topic area or theme, for example holidays, work, food.

Of course each interview will be different for each student or group of students, but a *typical* interview is described below.

★ At the start of the interview you will be asked to talk about one of the photographs among the Interview Exercises at the back of the book.

★ You will then be asked to discuss one of the passages at the back of the book. Your teacher may ask you to talk about its content, where you think it comes from, who the author or speaker is, whether you agree or disagree with it, and so on. You will *not* be asked to read the passage aloud, but you may quote parts of it to make your point.

★ You may then be asked to discuss for example an advertisement, a leaflet, extract from a newspaper etc. Your teacher will tell you which of the Interview Exercises to look at.

★ You may also be asked to take part in an activity with a group of other students or your teacher. Your teacher will tell you which section among the Interview Exercises you should look at.

Practice Test 3

PAPER 1   READING COMPREHENSION   (1 hour)

Answer all questions. Indicate your choice of answer in every case **on the separate answer sheet** *already given out, which should show your name and examination index number. Follow carefully the instructions about how to record your answers. Give* **one answer only** *to each question. Marks will not be deducted for wrong answers: your total score on this test will be the number of correct answers you give.*

SECTION A

In this section you must choose the word or phrase which best completes each sentence. **On your answer sheet** *indicate the letter A, B, C, or D against the number of each item 1 to 25 for the word or phrase you choose.*

1   Please accept our .... congratulations!
    A finest   B warmest   C dearest   D deepest

2   I'd sooner they .... deliver the new furniture tomorrow.
    A shouldn't   B didn't   C wouldn't   D mustn't

3   This film .... several scenes which are very funny.
    A features   B pictures   C depicts   D illustrates

4   Sales of margarine rose last year .... those of butter.
    A comparing   B at a loss of   C at the expense of   D with regard to

5   She should have been here but she's .... flu.
    A gone through with   B gone down with   C come in for
    D come up against

6   We all feel that his jokes about immigrants were in very poor ....
    A form   B view   C feeling   D taste

7   As the President was absent, I was asked to .... the meeting.
    A officiate   B govern   C chair   D regulate

8   The product was withdrawn from sale because there was no longer any
    .... for it.
    A call   B interest   C claim   D order

9 The trouble with Stan is that he makes such a fuss about even the most
.... injury.
A slight   B trivial   C basic   D elementary

10 I had no chance to defend myself: the dog .... for me as soon as I
opened the door.
A went   B ran   C fell   D stood

11 Please .... a copy of your application form for at least six months.
A return   B revise   C retain   D refer

12 As there is no-one to help them, the old couple have to .... for
themselves.
A fend   B look   C work   D rely

13 They turned down the proposal .... that it didn't fulfil their
requirements.
A by reason   B on the grounds   C as a cause   D allowing

14 Feeling very annoyed, I went for a swim largely as a means of letting off
....
A smoke   B temper   C anger   D steam

15 Sales reached a .... in June and then fell off.
A climax   B summit   C peak   D height

16 Get him to sign the contract before he has second ....
A plans   B thoughts   C intentions   D ideas

17 Tim was .... on causing mischief and nothing was going to stop him.
A intent   B determined   C fixed   D obsessed

18 He muttered something under his .... , but I didn't catch what he said.
A mouth   B breath   C voice   D chin

19 How exactly did you set .... training the horses to work so well
together?
A up   B to   C about   D out

20 If you're at a(n) .... end, you could help me in the garden.
A open   B free   C loose   D empty

21 He agreed to accept the position .... that he would be given a share of
the company's profits.
A in the agreement   B with the aim   C with the purpose
D on the understanding

22 This calculator has a number of .... in the way it can be used.

    A reservations   B constrictions   C obstructions   D limitations

23 I could tell at a .... that nothing had changed between Barbara and Edward.

    A glimpse   B blink   C wink   D glance

24 The new road currently under .... will solve the traffic problems in the town.

    A design   B progress   C construction   D work

25 I must get to bed early tonight; I sat up till the .... hours to finish that report.

    A small   B late   C deep   D last

SECTION B

In this section you will find after each of the passages a number of questions or unfinished statements about the passage, each with four suggested answers or ways of finishing. You must choose the one which you think fits best. **On your answer sheet, indicate the letter A, B, C or D against the number of each item 26–40 for the answer you choose. Give one answer only** *to each question. Read each passage right through before choosing your answers.*

FIRST PASSAGE

As I watch my contemporaries go into supposed retirement, am I the only one who gets fed up with hearing them say, 'Never been busier in my life'? What happened to that idyll of mellow old people enjoying their leisure, at last reading the books and following the hobbies they've longed to pursue, travelling without haste to distant places, occasionally giving the young their friendly wisdom and advice? Eminent speakers do their best to encourage the oldies. The Third Age, they maintain, offers an interesting opportunity: the postscript to the long letter of life; it is, or could be, the final glorious paragraph. But many people on the brink of retirement seem to regard it as more like a hectic footnote to fill up any space at the bottom of the page. And as for choosing what to do with their time, they seem terrified of it.

It's the supposedly successful people who are the most worried: and they see the ultimate success as not needing to retire at all. They become still more obsessed with the old game of filling up their diaries ('I might be able to squeeze you in in September'); and they prefer to measure their time in minutes rather than days.

It's not the actual busy-ness that bothers me. Everyone, of course, is entitled to be as busy as he likes in his own way. No, it's the insistence on being important in the conventional ways – sitting on company boards, collecting committees, having power-lunches or influential dinners. They must hang on, at all costs. If the demand doesn't really exist, they seem determined to create it, and fix the system to provide their own after-care service. Is there a new conference centre, an international institute, another advisory body to save the world? What more natural than to lobby for old Sir Whatsisname to run it – even if he does muddle up Bangkok with Bangalore, and repeat his jokes five minutes later?

The real power barons, who chair the boards or finance the institutes, often prefer to have old men around them. It's not necessarily because they bring wisdom and independent minds. It's sometimes – it must be said – for the opposite reason: because they are more anxious than anyone to hang on to their jobs. So the young have to give way to an older man.

Of course, they will say to me, it's all right for you writer fellows who can go on quietly boring your readers for years. You were never very responsibly employed in the first place, so you will hardly notice the difference. In government or business circles, they tell you, responsibility is much more serious and retirement is something much more terrible. One day we are feared and flattered, and everyone laughs at our jokes, the next day people don't even recognise us when we walk down the street without a car. So of course we must be found another job as soon as possible. The dread of retirement seems more serious at the top end of the market than at the bottom; and money seems to make it still worse. In fact I'm now told that the people we should most sympathise with are the *poor new rich*, who have retired early with a golden handshake. 'It's terrible to watch,' I was told by a stockbroker. 'Many of my clients were made redundant at 50, with a million or two. They looked forward to their life in their dream house in the country. And then their friends go back to work and they've suddenly got nothing whatever to do. If they weren't rich, they'd have to get some job, but they've got enough money to be able to bore themselves into the grave. And they may have another 30 years to go.'

26   The writer is annoyed by retired contemporaries who
     A   only pretend to have stopped working.
     B   insist on working after retirement age.
     C   confine themselves to selfish pleasure.
     D   are disenchanted by increased leisure opportunities.

27   In the writer's opinion, what seems to worry people as they reach retirement?
     A   how to spend their time
     B   losing their financial security
     C   not having enough time to fulfil their plans
     D   the fact that their life is drawing to a close

28 What do some older people try to create a demand for?
    A more conferences on issues concerning the elderly
    B new international charity organisations
    C the particular skills that they possess
    D their wide knowledge of current affairs

29 Why do some important men choose older advisers?
    A because they are reputed to be wise
    B because they are not influenced by modern trends
    C because they are unlikely to be ambitious for themselves
    D because they will do anything to keep their jobs

30 The writer of the passage earns his living as
    A a politician.
    B a diplomat.
    C a businessman.
    D an author.

31 Why, in the passage, are some rich people who retire early often
    disillusioned?
    A They regret moving to the country.
    B They dream about returning to work.
    C Retirement doesn't live up to their expectations.
    D Their friends lose interest in them.

SECOND PASSAGE

Opera is expensive: that much is inevitable. But expensive things are not inevitably the province of the rich unless we abdicate society's power of choice. We can choose to make opera, and other expensive forms of culture, accessible to those who cannot individually pay for it. The question is: why should we? Nobody denies the imperatives of food, shelter, defence, health and education. But even in a prehistoric cave, mankind stretched out a hand not just to eat, drink or fight, but also to draw. The impulse towards culture, the desire to express and explore the world through imagination and representation is fundamental. In Europe, this desire has found fulfilment in the masterpieces of our music, art, literature and theatre. These master-pieces are the touchstones for all our efforts; they are the touchstones for the possibilities to which human thought and imagination may aspire; they carry the most profound messages that can be sent from one human to another.

      What would we think of a society which did not attempt to teach its children about these achievements? And what would those children think if, having learnt that Mozart was one of the greatest creative minds who had ever lived, they discovered that his works were denied to all but those who passed the test of being rich?

Nobody should denigrate the value of the patronage of the rich. It is one of the great traditions of our culture, and the desire and the ability to beautify your life and your surroundings at your own expense is a noble one. But in method, taste and consumption, it is individual and private, and thus at odds with the fundamental nature of music, theatre and opera, which is public and communal.

Theatre sprang out of a need to dramatise the unknowable. We learn from a handful of human beings, most born without exceptional material privileges, that theatre can aspire to a genuinely profound and mystical experience. When the people of a city gather together in the darkness and immerse themselves collectively in the works of Mozart and Verdi, they are not only imbibing these great spirits for themselves but in concert with their unknown neighbours on either side. This is a profound social activity, which is by no means to be compared with sitting in isolation listening to a reproduction. The great spiritual force of the highest forms of theatre, music and opera stems from its ability to inspire an audience to feelings which are generously and publicly expressed, not harboured secretly and privately.

The civilised society will make music, theatre and opera the province of all its people. An uncivilised society reserves such achievements for a privileged few. The rest of society may learn about the existence of these achievements, but denied access to them, they will tend to hate the ideals and aspirations they embody, and ultimately, hate society itself. It is simply a question of choice.

32 The writer believes that since opera is expensive
    A people should be charged the full cost to see it.
    B only people who can afford it should see it.
    C it is unreasonable to expect it to become a popular art form.
    D society should give those with little money a chance to see it.

33 According to the writer, the opportunity to see opera is important because
    A the productions are spectacular.
    B opera combines music and theatre in a unique way.
    C the experience is the same for every generation.
    D opera embodies certain cultural values.

34 What criticism does the writer make of the patronage of the rich?
    A It is a way of showing off their status.
    B It is against the spirit of opera.
    C It is an outdated tradition.
    D It has affected the development of opera.

35 The theatre is a good place to enjoy music because
   A you are listening to an original performance.
   B you are actively taking part yourself.
   C you can appreciate the sounds and colours.
   D you are sharing an experience with other people.

36 In the author's opinion, the mark of a civilised society is that
   A it can produce sophisticated entertainment.
   B things of value are available to all.
   C everyone can be creative.
   D it has no privileged minority.

THIRD PASSAGE

The translator must have an excellent, up-to-date knowledge of his source languages, full facility in the handling of his target language, which will be his mother tongue or language of habitual use, and a knowledge and understanding of the latest subject-matter in his fields of specialisation. This is, as it were, his professional equipment. In addition to this, it is desirable that he should have an enquiring mind, wide interests, a good memory and the ability to grasp quickly the basic principles of new developments. He should be willing to work on his own, often at high speeds, but should be humble enough to consult others should his own knowledge not always prove adequate to the task in hand. He should be able to type fairly quickly and accurately and, if he is working mainly for publication, should have more than a nodding acquaintance with printing techniques and proof-reading. If he is working basically as an information translator, let us say, for an industrial firm, he should have the flexibility of mind to enable him to switch rapidly from one source language to another, as well as from one subject-matter to another, since this ability is frequently required of him in such work. Bearing in mind the nature of the translator's work, i.e. the processing of the written word, it is, strictly speaking, unnecessary that he should be able to speak the languages he is dealing with. If he does speak them, it is an advantage rather than a hindrance, but this skill is in many ways a luxury that he can dispense with. It is, however, desirable that he should have an approximate idea about the pronunciation of his source languages, even if this is restricted to knowing how proper names and place names are pronounced. The same applies to an ability to write his source languages. If he can, well and good; if he cannot, it does not matter. There are many other skills and qualities that are desirable in a translator.

»»→

37 The source language should be
    A the translator's native language.
    B the translator's language of habitual use.
    C a language the translator speaks as well as his mother tongue.
    D a language the translator is proficient in.

38 Which description of a translator would fit the author's requirements?
    A He is a slow but thorough worker.
    B He has contacts in printing and publishing.
    C He has good social skills.
    D He is well acquainted with his subject.

39 Why is humility desirable in a translator?
    A because he must not impose his views on a translation
    B because he will be more faithful to the text
    C because he may sometimes need to accept help from others
    D because he will put up with being left alone

40 Some good translators do not speak the languages they translate because
    A they are concerned with the written word.
    B they never meet the authors.
    C this allows them to work more efficiently.
    D this saves them expense during training.

PAPER 2   COMPOSITION   (2 hours)

*Write **two only** of the following composition exercises. Your answers must follow
exactly the instructions given. Write in pen, not pencil. You are allowed to make
alterations, but make sure that your work is clear and easy to read.*

1   Describe how the different personalities of your friends are reflected in the
    ways in which they spend their leisure time. (About 350 words)

2   'The world may be getting smaller but nations are no closer to
    understanding one another.' Do you agree or disagree with this statement?
    (About 350 words)

3   Write a story that begins with these words:
    'It was the most difficult decision anyone could be asked to make. Loyalty to
    the job and to the family were in conflict and there was very little time
    left . . .' (About 350 words)

4   You work for a tourist office and regularly stay in hotels in order to assess
    their facilities. Using the checklist below as a basis, write a report on your
    recent stay at the Hotel Grove for your office manager. (About 300 words)

Dear Guest,
Welcome to our hotel! We hope that you will enjoy your stay with us.

HOTEL GROVE

How were you served by our employees? 😊 😐 🙁

– Reception desk	○	○	✓
– Breakfast	✓	○	○
– Chambermaids, porters	○	✓	○
– Night porter	○	○	✓
–	○	○	○

Were you satisfied with the quality of what we offered?

– Room fittings, comfort	○	○	✓
– Bed	○	✓	○
– Mini-bar	✓	○	○
– Breakfast	✓	○	○

What was lacking in your room?
TV
Radio

Was anything in your room not working?
Shower

What is the reason for your stay?
– Holidays   ○
– Business   ✓

55

5   Basing your answer on your reading of the prescribed text concerned,
    answer **one** of the following. (About 350 words)

ERNEST HEMINGWAY: *A Farewell to Arms*
'Hemingway depicts the fear, the chaos, the comradeship and the courage
with total conviction.' Are these the most important aspects of the story in
your opinion?

OSCAR WILDE: *The Importance of Being Earnest*
Do you think that the play is very artificial or do you find the events and the
characters believable?

RUTH RENDELL: *A Judgement in Stone*
How far does the fact that Eunice cannot read explain her actions in
A Judgement in Stone?

PAPER 3   USE OF ENGLISH   (2 hours)

SECTION A

1   *Fill each of the numbered blanks in the passage with* **one** *suitable word.*

Homeopathy is essentially a natural healing process, providing remedies to assist the patient to regain health by stimulating the body's natural forces (1) .... recovery. It (2) .... on treating the patient, (3) .... than the disease.

For many years, homeopathic medicines have been recognised (4) .... a safe and effective method of treating ailments. Indeed, the (5) .... of homeopathy – that like cures like – has been known from the (6) .... of the ancient Greeks. Today it has been (7) .... in many countries to the point (8) .... it is formally accepted as a safe and effective alternative form of medical treatment.

There are many traditional homeopathic remedies (9) .... the treatment of winter ailments (10) .... as colds, coughs and influenza, and headaches and migraine can be treated by similar (11) .... Homeopathic medicines, which are (12) .... mainly from plants, are non-toxic and non-addictive, and have a major (13) .... in having no-side effects, (14) .... means they can be given safely in the (15) .... of children as well as of adults. (16) .... the past, homeopathic remedies were often produced in the home, (17) .... now commercial companies manufacture the products in licensed laboratories, to stringent (18) .... of quality. The medicines are often sold in tablet (19) .... , which (20) .... them easy to take.

2 *Finish each of the following sentences in such a way that it is as similar as possible in meaning to the sentence printed before it.*

EXAMPLE: I expect that he will get there by lunchtime.

ANSWER: I expect him *to get there by lunchtime.*

a) Alice and Charles did not decide to move to a bigger house until after the birth of their second child.

Only when ....

....

b) You're under no obligation to accept their offer.

You can please ....

c) Martin may not be very well but he still manages to enjoy life.

Martin's poor ....

....

d) The company presents a gold watch to each of its retiring employees.

Each ....

....

e) The only thing that kept us out of prison was the way he spoke the local dialect.

But for his command ....

....

f) The Pacific Ocean is on average deeper than the Atlantic.

The average ....

....

g) My father finds maps hard to follow.

My father has ....

h) Under no circumstances should you phone the police.

The last ....

3   *Fill each of the blanks with a suitable word or phrase.*

EXAMPLE: He doesn't mind one way or the other; it makes *no difference to* him.

a)   Your photograph doesn't stand .... winning first prize in that competition.

b)   How on earth .... lied to your best friend?

c)   We had a beautiful day for our picnic. The weather simply .... better.

d)   After the child had torn the book, the mother .... but to buy it.

e)   Had .... your help, I would never have managed to complete the course.

f)   Jim's aunt bought him books on astronomy and football, ... he had the slightest interest in.

4   *For each of the sentences below, write a new sentence* **as similar as possible in meaning to the original sentence** *but using the word given. This word* **must not be altered in any way**.

EXAMPLE: Not many people attended the meeting.
turnout

ANSWER: *There was a poor turnout for the meeting.*

a)   People don't want to buy cars with large engines any more.
call

....

....

b)   Twenty years ago this region produced twice as much coal as it does now.
halved

....

....

c) The Prime Minister is unlikely to call an early general election.
   likelihood

   ....

   ....

d) Nobody could possibly believe the story he told us.
   beyond

   ....

e) The project received the unanimous approval of the committee.
   favour

   ....

   ....

f) Scientists say forests are being destroyed by air pollution.
   blame

   ....

   ....

g) His reactions are quite unpredictable.
   knows

   ....

h) There are several categories of people who do not have to pay the new tax.
   exempt

   ....

   ....

SECTION B

5 *Read the following passage, then answer the questions which follow it.*

The Meaning of Competition

In contemporary Western culture there is a great deal of controversy about competition. One segment values it highly, believing that it is responsible for Western progress and prosperity. Another segment says that competition is bad; that it pits one person against another and is therefore divisive; that it leads to enmity between people and therefore 5 to a lack of co-operation and eventual ineffectualness. Those who value competition believe in sports such as football, baseball, tennis and golf. Those who see competition as a form of legalised hostility tend to favour such non-competitive forms of recreation as surfing or jogging.

I have taught many children and teenagers who were caught up in 10 the belief that their self-worth depended on how well they performed at tennis and other skills. For them, playing well and winning are often life-and-death issues. In their single-minded pursuit of measurable success, the development of many other human potentialities is sadly neglected. 15

But whereas some seem to get trapped in the compulsion to succeed, others take a rebellious stance. Pointing to the limitations involved in a cultural pattern which tends to value only the winner and ignore even the positive of the mediocre, they vehemently criticise competition. Among the most vocal are youngsters who have suffered 20 under competitive pressures imposed on them by parents or society. Teaching these young people, I often observe in them a desire to fail. They seem to seek failure by making no effort to win or achieve success. They go on strike, as it were. By not trying, they always have an alibi: 'I may have lost, but it doesn't count because I really didn't try.' What is 25 not usually admitted is the belief that if they had really tried and lost, then yes, that *would* count. Such a loss would be a measure of their worth. Clearly, this belief is the same as that of the competitor trying to prove himself. Both are based on the mistaken assumption that one's sense of self-respect rides on how well one performs in relation to 30 others. Both are afraid of not measuring up. Only as this fundamental and often nagging fear begins to dissolve can we discover a new meaning in competition.

My own attitude toward competition went through quite an evolution before I arrived at my present point of view. I was raised to believe 35 in competition, and both playing well and winning meant a great deal to me. But as I began applying the principles of yoga to the teaching and playing of tennis, I became non-competitive. Instead of trying to win, I decided to attempt only to play beautifully and excellently. My idea was

to be unconcerned with how well I was doing in relation to my 40
opponent and absorbed solely in achieving excellence for its own sake.
Very beautiful, I would waltz around the court being very fluid, accurate
and 'wise'.

But something was missing. I didn't experience a desire to win, and
as a result I often lacked the necessary determination. One day I had an 45
interesting experience which convinced me in an unexpected way that
playing for the sake of beauty and excellence was not all there was to
tennis. Just before a game, I received a phone call, telling me that an
important engagement had been cancelled. The excuse was a valid one
and the person was so nice that I couldn't get angry, but as I hung up I 50
realised I was furious. I grabbed my racket, ran down to the tennis court
and began hitting balls harder than I ever had before. Amazingly, most
of them went in. I didn't let up when the match began, nor did I relent
my all-out attack until it was over. Even on crucial points I would go for
winning shots and make them. I was playing with an uncharacteristic 55
determination even when ahead; in fact I was playing *out of my mind*.
Somehow the anger had taken me beyond my own preconceived
limitations; it took me beyond caution.

But anger couldn't be the secret to great tennis, or could it? I hadn't
been angry at my opponent or at myself. I was simply furious in such a 60
way that it took me out of my mind. It enabled me to play with abandon,
unconcerned about winning or playing well. I just hit the ball, and
enjoyed it! It was one of the most fulfilling times I'd ever had on the
court. Paradoxically, winning at that point didn't matter to me, but I
found myself making my greatest effort. 65

a) Explain in your own words why some people 'value' competition
   'highly'. (line 2)

   ....

   ....

b) Explain in your own words 'it pits one person against another'. (line 4)

   ....

c) What is the final product of competition, according to its critics?
   (lines 5–6)

   ....

d) What does the writer mean by 'legalised hostility'? (line 8)

   ....

e) Which phrase in the second paragraph underlines the importance of success to some children?

   ....

f) Explain in your own words the danger children face in the 'single-minded pursuit of measurable success'. (lines 13–14)

   ....

   ....

g) According to the writer, how does society regard the performance of those who do not win?

   ....

   ....

h) What does the writer mean by 'the most vocal'? (line 20)

   ....

i) Explain how a 'desire to fail' (line 22) can act as an alibi.

   ....

   ....

   ....

j) In your own words, explain the similarity between true competitors and those with a 'desire to fail'.

   ....

   ....

k) Explain the phrase a 'nagging fear'. (line 32)

   ....

l) Explain why the writer was not satisfied with playing beautifully.

   ....

   ....

m) How is the phrase 'out of one's mind' normally used?

   ....

≫→

n) What does 'I was playing *out of my mind*' mean in line 56?

....

....

o) In your own words, explain the paradox referred to in lines 64–65.

....

....

p) In a paragraph of 70–90 words, summarise the ways in which concentrating on winning can be disadvantageous.

....

....

....

....

....

....

....

....

....

....

....

....

....

PAPER 4   LISTENING COMPREHENSION
(about 30 minutes)

PART ONE

You will hear two people talking about teaching. They begin by discussing whether teachers should go on strike. For questions 1–7 indicate the correct answer by putting a tick in the box next to the appropriate letter.

1   What does the teacher think about teachers striking?

   A He thinks it is a good thing.

   B He regrets it.

   C He disapproves of it.

   D He thinks it is unavoidable.

A	
B	
C	
D	

2   During the last ten years

   A teachers' wages have been cut in real terms.

   B teachers' wages have remained the same.

   C teachers' wages have been overtaken by other professions.

   D teachers' wages have kept pace with other professions.

A	
B	
C	
D	

3   What does the woman say a lot of parents think?

   A Teachers get good wages.

   B Teachers have an easy job.

   C Teachers often don't do a good job.

   D Teachers have plenty of free time.

A	
B	
C	
D	

4   Which of the following duties does the teacher consider most important?

A assessment of one's own work

B preparing day-to-day materials

C carrying out administrative duties

D evaluating one's colleagues' work

A	
B	
C	
D	

5   According to the teacher, holidays offer the chance to

A advance new educational ideas.

B study for more qualifications.

C take a spare-time job.

D catch up on outstanding work.

A	
B	
C	
D	

6   When the teacher talks about holidays does he sound

A confident?

B hesitant?

C defensive?

D confused?

A	
B	
C	
D	

7   How does the teacher feel about teaching?

A conscientious

B depressed

C indifferent

D enthusiastic

A	
B	
C	
D	

PART TWO

You will hear two people talking about a film, which one of them has seen. For questions 8–11 indicate the correct answer by putting a tick in the box next to the appropriate letter.

8 How did the man feel about the film?

   A He thought it was visually impressive.

   B He enjoyed it more as it went on.

   C He thought the acting was stiff and unnatural.

   D He regretted going to see it.

A	
B	
C	
D	

9 How did the man feel about the book on which the film was based?

   A He wasn't very keen on it.

   B He thought it unrealistic.

   C He thought it was too sensational.

   D He felt sure it would make a good film.

A	
B	
C	
D	

10 What was the woman's reaction to seeing the trailer?

   A She decided not to see the film.

   B She felt the film bore no resemblance to the book.

   C She objected to part of the plot being omitted.

   D She felt the mystical elements were inadequately dealt with.

A	
B	
C	
D	

11 How does the man feel about the way Dr Aziz is portrayed in the film?

   A The character is not presented clearly.

   B He is no more than a caricature.

   C The sudden change in him is well acted.

   D He is developed in a believable way.

A	
B	
C	
D	

PART THREE

*You will hear part of an interview with a woman called Adela Boden, who has been teaching at a girls' boarding school in Ghana. For questions **12–16**, indicate the correct answer by putting a tick in the box next to the appropriate letter.*

12 Adela Boden found that a Ghanaian boarding school

A took girls from many different ethnic backgrounds.

B was run on cosmopolitan lines.

C provided an international working atmosphere.

D offered a wide mix of cultural activities.

A	
B	
C	
D	

13 The girls at the school taught the speaker

A how to organise her home life.

B how to spend her leisure time.

C to appreciate Ghanaian customs.

D to enjoy Ghanaian food.

A	
B	
C	
D	

14 By the time Adela returned to Europe she had

A acquired a knowledge of Ghanaian music.

B recorded a music programme for Ghanaians.

C been shown how to play Ghanaian drums.

D learnt how to harmonise Ghanaian songs.

A	
B	
C	
D	

15 What does Adela say about the way the Ghanaian climate affected her?

A She had to take extra rest during the long, hot mornings.

B She needed frequent baths to cope with perspiration.

C She found running to and from lessons kept her fit.

D She was obliged to reassess the rate at which she did things.

A	
B	
C	
D	

16   What does the speaker say about the initial part of her life in Ghana?

A Travelling around was very exciting.	A
B She found life too demanding.	B
C She longed for news from home.	C
D She felt very lonely.	D

PART FOUR

You will hear a woman called Jenny describing her job as an occupational therapist. Look at the list of possible requirements for the job, numbered 17–23. Show which of them apply to Jenny's particular post by indicating YES or NO. Put a tick in the appropriate box.

We wish to appoint an Occupational Therapist. The successful applicant will:

	YES	NO
17 be based at a local hospital.		
18 visit people in their own homes.		
19 be involved in the running of a home for the elderly.		
20 work with people of all age groups.		
21 be required to work closely with the management.		
22 give advice to patients.		
23 provide specialist advice.		

PAPER 5 INTERVIEW (15–20 minutes)

You will be asked to take part in a conversation with a group of other students or with your teacher. The conversation will be based on one particular topic area or theme, for example holidays, work, food.

Of course each interview will be different for each student or group of students, but a *typical* interview is described below.

★ At the start of the interview you will be asked to talk about one of the photographs among the Interview Exercises at the back of the book.

★ You will then be asked to discuss one of the passages at the back of the book. Your teacher may ask you to talk about its content, where you think it comes from, who the author or speaker is, whether you agree or disagree with it, and so on. You will *not* be asked to read the passage aloud, but you may quote parts of it to make your point.

★ You may then be asked to discuss for example an advertisement, a leaflet, extract from a newspaper etc. Your teacher will tell you which of the Interview Exercises to look at.

★ You may also be asked to take part in an activity with a group of other students or your teacher. Your teacher will tell you which section among the Interview Exercises you should look at.

Practice Test 4

PAPER 1   READING COMPREHENSION   (1 hour)

Answer all questions. Indicate your choice of answer in every case **on the separate answer sheet** *already given out, which should show your name and examination index number. Follow carefully the instructions about how to record your answers. Give* **one answer only** *to each question. Marks will not be deducted for wrong answers: your total score on this test will be the number of correct answers you give.*

SECTION A

In this section you must choose the word or phrase which best completes each sentence. **On your answer sheet** *indicate the letter A, B, C or D against the number of each item 1 to 25 for the word or phrase you choose.*

1   It is difficult for museums to find funds to protect the nation's ....
    A inheritance   B heritage   C possessions   D legacy

2   He could provide no documentary evidence to .... up his claim that dinosaurs had once inhabited these hills.
    A back   B fill   C make   D hold

3   From an early lead, the team .... to an embarrassing defeat.
    A slumped   B fell   C declined   D dropped

4   All the applicants for the post are thoroughly .... for their suitability.
    A searched   B investigated   C vetted   D scrutinised

5   She expressed her .... for certain kinds of cheaply produced movies.
    A disapproval   B distaste   C dissatisfaction   D disloyalty

6   The life of a spy is .... with danger.
    A fraught   B intense   C stressful   D heavy

7   'I think we ought to see the rest of the exhibition as quickly as we can, ... that it closes in half an hour.'
    A granted   B assuming   C given   D knowing

8   Because of road works, traffic is restricted to one .... in each direction.
    A lane   B row   C alley   D path

9   The film star .... his intention of going into politics.
     A showed   B demanded   C gave   D indicated

10   Pedestrians are advised to cross the road by means of the ....
     A bypass   B subway   C underground   D footpath

11   The farmer decided to .... his claims to the disputed land in the courts.
     A pursue   B follow   C secure   D chase

12   Although I had only just met them, the Johnsons .... me like a friend.
     A knew   B kept   C estimated   D treated

13   They've bought a holiday cottage near the sea, and in .... course they
     plan to move there permanently.
     A due   B future   C coming   D intended

14   Beaches were .... as police searched for canisters of toxic waste from
     the damaged ship.
     A sealed off   B cut off   C washed up   D kept out

15   It was agreed that the contract would be renewed .... to certain
     changes.
     A liable   B subject   C responsive   D according

16   The athlete's injury occurred when she was at the .... of physical
     fitness.
     A zenith   B top   C peak   D summit

17   Windows go .... towards defining the character of a house.
     A a long way   B far out   C all the way   D far away

18   .... the public's concern about the local environment, this new road
     scheme will have to be abandoned.
     A As regards   B In view of   C In the event of   D However much

19   Ellen decided that election to the local council would provide a .... to a
     career in national politics.
     A springboard   B turning-point   C milestone   D highway

20   One year after the fraud was discovered, there is still little .... of any
     money being recovered.
     A demonstration   B sign   C token   D manifestation

21   Norman .... himself on his careful driving.
     A pleases   B prides   C comments   D boasts

22 Jonathan took over the manager's job, ... when Mr Thomas retired.
   A left   B emptied   C vacated   D resigned

23 If the number of berries on the holly tree is anything to .... , we are
   likely to have a hard winter.
   A look at   B go by   C point on   D think about

24 The workers voted in favour of a(n) .... strike.
   A interminable   B endless   C ceaseless   D indefinite

25 The air in the town centre was .... with petrol fumes.
   A strong   B thick   C full   D unpleasant

SECTION B

In this section you will find after each of the passages a number of questions or unfinished statements about the passage, each with four suggested answers or ways of finishing. You must choose the one which you think fits best. **On your answer sheet, indicate the letter A, B, C or D against the number of each item 26–40 for the answer you choose. Give one answer only** *to each question. Read each passage right through before choosing your answers.*

FIRST PASSAGE

Cuisine and probably also music are the most accessible parts of a culture and, at the same time, the most resistant to outside influence. They are the first points of real physical contact with a different society. Part of knowing how to travel is to have an appreciation for other cuisines: this is still one of the rare ways in which people of different backgrounds can learn easily from each other.

It is in this sense that I am interested in other cuisines. In more than fifteen years of travelling over the last quarter of a century, I have had direct experience (in on-the-spot investigation and by studying both political struggles and poetry) of societies in the Middle East, South-East Asia, Africa, Europe and the Americas. I have tried over the years to capture as much as possible of their 'differences', and among them the difference between cuisines: this is the very essence of the pleasure of travelling. Almost everywhere I have learned how to make the local dishes that most appealed to me.

Cuisine is an art which (discounting a handful of outstanding professionals) has always been developed by amateurs or, to be more precise, by professionals who have never been recognised as such because they were women. Perhaps most of the European cuisine of the leisured classes of the nineteenth century is so unnecessarily complicated and pretentious

73

because it was elaborated by the great chefs. Elsewhere, even the most subtle cuisines, whether aristocratic or popular in origin, are relatively simple apart from a few dishes.

The art of cooking calls for a little patience, organisation and precision: that customary precision of traditional societies that seems so vague in quantified terms. It derives from an interest in the taste of food and the sheer delight of satisfying the guest. There is one other essential requirement: one must cook with natural foods.

The search for provisions, from indispensable staples to the luxury of spices, has shaped the development of human societies. Through the ages, the problems of food, whether of sheer necessity or of idle indulgence, have led to conflicts, growth, trade and the discovery of the New World. (All this time most of the world has been short of food, and will continue to be so.) The culinary heritage of the world, in the sense of *haute cuisine*, is, however, the product of abundance.

26 The author is interested in other cuisines because they are
   A material products of different cultures.
   B artistic endeavours in their own right.
   C essential for the traveller.
   D accessible to any traveller.

27 The author suggests that women cooks
   A are unprofessional.
   B have been undervalued.
   C do not take cooking seriously.
   D cannot compete with male chefs.

28 What style of cooking does the writer approve of?
   A nineteenth-century European
   B that developed by famous cooks
   C simple
   D popular

29 The precision demanded by traditional, non-European cuisines results from
   A careful measurements.
   B the local produce.
   C pleasure.
   D necessity.

30 The author argues that elaborate cuisines are a product of
   A world-wide trade.
   B luxuries such as spices.
   C a plentiful supply of foodstuffs.
   D the availability of leisure for all classes.

SECOND PASSAGE

Their first holiday since their honeymoon was paid for by the elderly man they both called Uncle. However, something went wrong with the booking, and Dawne and Keith ended up in Switzerland instead of Venice, which was where they had intended to go. Despite all manner of protests, they were completely unable to get transferred onwards.

It was not the first time Keith and Dawne had suffered in this way: they were familiar with defeat. There'd been the time, a couple of years after their marriage, when Keith had got into debt through purchasing materials for making ships in bottles; earlier – before they'd even met – there was the occasion when the Lamb and Flag pub had let Dawne go because she'd taken tips although the rules categorically forbade it. Once, Keith had sawn through the wrong water pipe and the landlords had come along with a bill for nearly two hundred pounds when the ceiling of the flat below collapsed. It was Uncle who had given Dawne a job in his shop after the Lamb and Flag episode and who had put them on their feet by paying off the arrears of the handicraft debt. In the end he persuaded them to come and live with him, pointing out that the arrangement would suit all three of them. Since his sister's death he had found it troublesome managing on his own.

In Interlaken they selected a postcard to send him: of a mountain that had featured in a James Bond film. But they didn't know what to write on it: if they told the truth they would receive the old man's unspoken scorn when they returned – a look that came into his eyes while he silently regarded them. Years ago he had openly said – once only – that they were accident-prone. They were unfortunate in their dealings with the world, he had explained when Dawne asked him; lame ducks, he supposed you could say, if they'd forgive the expression; victims by nature, no fault of their own. Ever since, such judgements had been expressed only through his eyes.

'A strike?' Dawne suggested. 'You're always hearing of strikes in airports.'

But Keith continued to gaze at the blank postcard, not persuaded that an attempt at falsehood was wise. It wasn't easy to tell the old man a lie. He had a way of making such attempts feel clumsy and, in the end, of winkling out the truth. Yet his scorn would continue for many months, especially since he had paid out what he would call, a couple of hundred times at least, 'good money' for their tickets. 'That's typical of Keith, that is,' he'd repeatedly inform his customers in Dawne's hearing, and she'd pass it on that night, the way she always passed his comments on.

31 Why did Keith and Dawne go to live with the old man?
   A He needed their assistance.
   B They couldn't afford to live on their own.
   C He offered Dawne a job.
   D They owed him money.

32 Keith and Dawne considered lying to the old man on the postcard because
    they didn't want him
    A to tell other people.
    B to worry about their situation.
    C to have his opinions confirmed.
    D to be disappointed.

33 What was the old man's view of Keith and Dawne?
    A They were not very sensible.
    B They were not responsible for their misfortune.
    C They should be more careful.
    D They took on overambitious projects.

34 Why did Keith not want to lie to the old man?
    A He couldn't think of a plausible story.
    B He felt Dawne's suggestion was unconvincing.
    C He thought the old man would see through it.
    D He believed it was morally wrong.

THIRD PASSAGE

Ever since the first newsphoto was made 140 years ago – a panoramic view
of Hamburg after the big fire of 1842 – photojournalism has excelled in
depicting horrors. The pleasant, the ordinary rarely make the news.
    Given the demand for sensational photographs, everyone regards press
photographers as an overbearing lot, as mercenaries in the pay of public
curiosity; ever in pursuit, flashgun at the ready, of the unsuspecting victim.
Armed to the teeth with the tools of their trade, they elbow their way
through the crowd, trampling on the gardens of the famous, jamming their
feet into half-closed doors and lying in wait for the widow before the
still-open grave. But are press photographers really only cold 'glass-
eyewitnesses'? Certainly, in talking to top photographers, the dilemma of
this profession comes out: how can artistic sensitivity be reconciled with
the necessarily tough job of the reporter?
    Philip Jones Griffiths, despite having produced the most terrifying
book of photographs on the Vietnam War ever seen and having been a
reporter for twenty years, still has difficulty in photographing people in the
street: 'If you are sensitive enough to see unusual images, you are also
sensitive and shy when you have to stick your lens into some stranger's
face.' Griffiths now knows instinctively how far he can go on each occasion.
He has learned to interpret the body language of the people around him and
achieves what he wants by gentle persuasion: 'So far I have never been
attacked. No one has ever thrown me out.'
    Volker Hinz, on the staff of the magazine *Stern*, is regarded by his
colleagues as a tough nut who never takes no for an answer. Yet he says for

himself, 'Deep down, I'm a shy person. It costs me a great deal of psychological effort to have to elbow my way through a crowd of photographers to get to the front. But what can you do? I have to get the best picture at all costs.' Hinz also knows that cold routine can be dangerous. 'I have to work up enthusiasm for each new job. I have to become more open and sensitive. I have to be prepared for the unexpected.'

Being up close – that is the curse but also the strength of the photographic medium. A reporter can do his writing from a safe distance behind the lines, gather information second-hand or even by sorting through files. A photographer has no choice; he cannot take photos from behind a desk, he has to be right where the action is. This requires a special temperament.

'Occasionally photographers are a little crazy, and almost always they are obsessed,' writes *Time* magazine in a story on photojournalism. Good photographers seldom fit the corporate mould. They can be a nuisance; most are emotional. Many of them are politically motivated and have a soft spot for the downtrodden, since every day they have to cross the line towards poverty, sickness, mischief or simply towards the everyday lives of the common mass. Photography is blue collar work. It means dragging heavy equipment around, rain or shine, in heat and cold; it means hanging out at street corners – certainly not a noble profession.

35 Press photographers are criticised in the second paragraph for
    A showing too much interest in money.
    B behaving in a military fashion.
    C carrying too much equipment.
    D showing no respect for other people.

36 A major problem which all press photographers face in their job is how to
    A gain access to important scenes.
    B cope with technical difficulties.
    C maintain a human outlook.
    D win the confidence of their subjects.

37 What does the passage tell us about Philip Jones Griffiths?
    A He finds some aspects of photography difficult.
    B His pictures cause offence.
    C His current work reflects his wartime experiences.
    D He prefers not to photograph people.

38 What disturbs Volker Hinz?
    A He worries that his behaviour may become too automatic.
    B He is frightened of missing the best pictures.
    C He feels his shyness is a weakness.
    D He is unhappy with people's view of him.

39 According to the writer, how does the job of a reporter compare with that of
    a press photographer?
    A It is less dangerous.
    B It allows more freedom.
    C It doesn't need such a strong character.
    D It is mostly based in the office.

40 According to the passage, what do good photographers often have in
    common?
    A They have a high opinion of themselves.
    B They have an individual outlook.
    C They will do anything to get a good photograph.
    D They are unmoved by the problems they photograph.

PAPER 2   COMPOSITION   (2 hours)

*Write **two only** of the composition exercises. Your answers must follow exactly the instructions given. Write in pen, not pencil. You are allowed to make alterations, but make sure that your work is clear and easy to read.*

1   Describe a newspaper or magazine with which you are familiar and explain why you think it is worth reading. (About 350 words)

2   'Everyday life is no longer possible without computers.' Do you agree? (About 350 words)

3   Write a story which begins: 'As soon as it was dark, I left the house to go to work knowing there would be trouble when I arrived.' (About 350 words)

4   Write a report of a proposal to build a new housing complex on the outskirts of a major town in your country. The report could include the following points: (About 300 words)
    – necessity
    – overcrowding
    – better facilities
    – environmental safeguards

5   Basing your answer on your reading of the prescribed text concerned, answer **one** of the following. (About 350 words)

    ERNEST HEMINGWAY: *A Farewell to Arms*
    Do you think that *A Farewell to Arms* is an appropriate title for the story? Give your reasons.

    OSCAR WILDE: *The Importance of Being Earnest*
    'The play is still amusing but the characters are no longer real.' Discuss.

    RUTH RENDELL: *A Judgement in Stone*
    What is the relevance to the story of Eunice's inability to read and write?

PAPER 3 USE OF ENGLISH (2 hours)

SECTION A

1 *Fill each of the numbered blanks in the passage with* **one** *suitable word.*

In our eyes, the desirability of a material or object is inextricably linked to its availability. If it is plentiful and therefore cheap, it becomes unattractive. It is (1) .... simple human truth that has brought (2) .... a reversal in the perception of plastics in the twentieth century. As the industrial uses (3) .... grown, the appreciation of plastics (4) .... materials having intrinsic beauty has (5) ....

Bakelite, a material discovered by L H Baekeland, typifies the changing attitude of the public (6) .... plastics. In the early (7) .... of its development, it was made (8) .... decorative objects and was used as a moulded substitute for onyx and marble. (9) .... demand grew, it was produced in greater (10) .... , became cheaper and began to be used for light-fittings, telephones and ashtrays, thus losing any pretensions to stylishness it (11) .... had. The same attitude (12) .... to all plastic nowadays, to the (13) .... that 'plasticky' has become a derogatory (14) .... even though many plastics are very expensive. Fluorocarbons in particular perform well in situations (15) .... no other material, (16) .... the cost, would be able to survive.

Because of this change (17) .... attitude, plastics are rarely used (18) .... purely aesthetic purposes. Although some beautiful products are still made, the sad (19) .... is that plastics are now usually chosen for the simple (20) .... that production is not feasible in any other material.

2 *Finish each of the following sentences in such a way that it is as similar as possible in meaning to the sentence printed before it.*

EXAMPLE: I expect that he will get there by lunchtime.

ANSWER: I expect him *to get there by lunchtime.*

a) The film star wore dark glasses so that no-one would recognise him.

The film star avoided ....

....

b) I am amazed by the mistakes he makes.

What ....

c) We weren't surprised by his success.

It came ....

d) 'That's a lovely new dress, Jean,' said her mother.

Jean's mother complimented ....

e) We couldn't relax until all the guests had gone home.

Only ....

....

f) We couldn't find George anywhere.

George was ....

g) Customs officials are stopping more travellers than usual this week.

An increased ....

....

h) She listens more sympathetically than anyone else I know.

She is a ....

....

3 *Fill each of the blanks with a suitable word or phrase.*

EXAMPLE: He doesn't mind one way or the other; it makes *no difference to* him.

a) 'You're late again! .... caught an earlier bus?'

b) 'If you don't stop the car at that red light, you .... the law.'

c) I am pleased to say that we've always .... terms with our neighbours.

d) When the fire started, Barbara was the first person .... the alarm.

e) Harry explained to the police that he had .... stolen.

f) 'It's high .... effort to look after yourself.'

4 *For each of the sentences below, write a new sentence* **as similar as possible in meaning to the original sentence** *but using the word given. This word* **must not be altered in any way.**

EXAMPLE: Not many people attended the meeting.
turnout

ANSWER: *There was a poor turnout for the meeting.*

a) The minister's popularity suffered as a result of the scandal.
effect

....

....

b) The teachers agreed to introduce the new methods.
agreement

....

....

c) Jenny didn't feel like going to the party.
mood

....

....

d) The councillor answered every question frankly.
    frank

    ....

    ....

e) It is said that he has been to prison several times.
    reputed

    ....

    ....

f) Most stores will accept a credit card instead of cash.
    alternative

    ....

    ....

g) Our opinions on the subject are identical.
    difference

    ....

    ....

h) Local residents said they were against the new traffic scheme.
    disapproval

    ....

    ....

SECTION B

5   *Read the following passage, then answer the questions which follow it.*

Old Age

In many cultures of the world the transition from adulthood to old age is
not seen, as it is in ours, as a lessening of activity, a retreat from social
usefulness. For the old there is still 'much to be done', much that needs
doing and much that they can do better than any others. Such societies

do not see old age as an end to life, but as a source of continuity, linking   5
the future with the past, death with life. This more positive attitude to
the aged does not necessarily demand a belief in after-life, or in God; it
depends simply upon the recognition of the vital role that old people
have to play in the ongoing life of their society.

In the Western world things are different. For all too many old   10
people here, the persistent reference to the 'golden years' of old age has
become a cruel hoax, a lie, a promise that can never be fulfilled. The
should-have-been-golden years are discovered instead to be a frightening ante-room to extinction, a time of loneliness and suffering, to be
postponed as long as possible. Compulsory retirement for many means   15
little more than compulsory unemployment, bringing with it not only
financial stress, but, far more significantly, a certain social stigma
associated with uselessness, incompetence and dependence, all the
more bitter and frustrating because it is compelled, unwanted and
totally unnecessary. Even when old age is accompanied by infirmity or   20
incapacity, the old have a wealth to give, and could contribute until the
very day of their death, as they do in other societies.

Just as each of the other four stages of life – childhood, adolescence,
youth, and adulthood – has its own special potential, its own contribution to make, so does old age. Far from being useless and unproductive,   25
the old in every society are a vital source of richness and strength. Their
way of contributing to the general good is often so subtle as to be almost
invisible, but it is nonetheless real and powerful. Certainly in other
cultures, particularly, perhaps, those with a firm belief in an after- or
other-life, the old are accorded a position of often enormous respect and   30
honour and are exploited for the social good until they die, when they
continue to be exploited as 'ancestors'. While alive their contribution
may be economic, for certain very practical skills come with old age. In
some societies the political role of the old is formalised, their long years
of experience being called on to help in the resolution of otherwise   35
intractable disputes. Having so little to gain or lose, the old make
admirable arbitrators. In a more general social role the old are vitally
important as educators, and we throw away this invaluable resource
every time we employ a baby-sitter only a few days older than the baby.
But then, in our society, we do not seem to place much value on   40
education, even in our school system, so our young are deprived of the
wonders that can be so easily passed on to them by that special, intimate
exchange that perhaps is only possible between the very young and the
very old. And so the old are deprived of yet another role. But most of all
they are ignored, in our society, for the very thing that makes them so   45
immensely powerful in other societies: their proximity to death. That is
perhaps what we most need to explore, this association in other cultures
of the old with that vast source of spirit power that lies beyond death. It
provides a whole new perspective on old age.

a) Explain in your own words how the change from adulthood to old age is seen in Western culture.

....

....

b) How does the role of old people in some societies reflect a 'more positive attitude'? (line 6)

....

....

c) Explain the phrase 'the persistent reference to the "golden years" of old age'. (line 11)

....

....

d) What does the writer mean by 'a frightening ante-room to extinction'? (lines 13–14)

....

....

e) What is the economic effect of compulsory retirement on the old?

....

f) What is 'frustrating' (line 19) and why?

....

....

g) In your own words, explain what old age has in common with 'the other four stages of life'. (line 23)

....

....

h) Why is the contribution of old people said to be 'so subtle as to be almost invisible'? (lines 27–28)

....

....

i) Why do the old in some societies continue to enjoy 'enormous respect and honour'? (lines 30–31)

....

....

j) What two characteristics make the old good judges in an argument?

....

....

k) To what is the writer referring in the phrase 'this invaluable resource'? (line 38)

....

....

l) Explain in your own words why Westerners are said to ignore the old.

....

....

m) What does the writer mean by 'a whole new perspective on old age'? (line 49)

....

....

n) In a paragraph of 70–90 words, explain how the old can be 'a vital source of richness and strength'. (line 26)

....

....

....

....

....

....

....

....

....

PAPER 4   LISTENING COMPREHENSION
(about 30 minutes)

PART ONE

You will hear a man from Central Europe talking about a tour of North America which he made after retiring. For questions 1–5 indicate the correct answer by putting a tick in the box next to the appropriate letter.

1   How does the speaker react to the idea of sudden retirement?

A He thinks it can bring on insomnia.

B He thinks it may contribute to an early death.

C He thinks it may cause depression.

D He thinks it can be hard to adjust to.

A	
B	
C	
D	

2   What attracted the speaker to travelling after retirement?

A He could travel right round the world.

B He wanted to pursue his leisure activities.

C He would have more time to explore.

D He wanted to sell his home.

A	
B	
C	
D	

3   Why didn't the speaker go to Australia?

A He preferred the political climate of the USA.

B He felt it was too far to go overland.

C He was deterred by political considerations.

D He was very keen to travel to the West.

A	
B	
C	
D	

4   Why did the speaker decide to spend three years in the USA?

A   He wanted to avoid travelling too far too quickly.

B   He decided to retrace early explorers' routes.

C   He needed time to adapt to another culture.

D   He felt the sheer size justified the time.

A	
B	
C	
D	

5   What does the speaker say about North American scenery?

A   The space and beauty are beyond description.

B   It is far more beautiful than European scenery.

C   The emptiness and lack of habitation are frightening.

D   It offers an escape from overpopulated countries.

A	
B	
C	
D	

PART TWO

You will hear an interview between a prospective employer and someone who runs a recruitment agency. Look at the form below. For questions **6–15** *indicate the correct answer by ticking the appropriate response or, for questions* **12** *and* **13**, *by writing a short answer.*

TROUBLE SHOOTERS RECRUITMENT
(Domestic Section)

Name: *Mrs J Saunders*
Address   *Dovers Farmhouse WESTEND Nr Appledown   Phone 0711-6563*

REQUIREMENTS:

6   **A**   Full-time living in ☐
    B   Part-time living in ☐
    C   Full-time living out ☐
    D   Part-time living out ☐

7   **A**   Nanny ☐
    B   Nanny for newborn ☐
    C   Au pair ☐
    D   General help, no children ☐
    E   General help, house and children ☐
    F   Cleaning only ☐

TROUBLE SHOOTERS RECRUITMENT
(Domestic Section) continued

8   Driving licence   YES / NO

ACCOMMODATION:

9   **A** Rural ☐
     B Urban ☐

10 **A** Own flat/cottage ☐
     B Own room and bath ☐
     C Own room ☐

11 **A** Meals with family ☐
     B Meals provided ☐
     C Do own cooking ☐
     D No meals ☐

FAMILY DETAILS:

12 Adults: ....

13 Children: ....

14 Responsibility for children:
     A At all times ☐
     B In parents' absence only ☐
     C Shared with parents ☐

15 Corporal punishment:
     A Prohibited ☐
     B Parents only ☐
     C Allowed ☐

PART THREE

You will hear part of a radio programme in which a doctor talks about jet lag. For questions 16–25, indicate whether you think each statement is TRUE or FALSE by putting a tick in the appropriate box.

According to the doctor:

	True	False
16 You really only suffer from jet lag when you fly east.		
17 The problem of jet lag is that many people become hyperactive.		
18 Only certain people suffer from jet lag.		
19 Jet lag affects young children less.		
20 If you are flying west you can reduce the effects of jet lag before you go by going to bed and getting up later.		
21 If you are flying east you can reduce the effects of jet lag before you go by having your meals later.		
22 It's better not to sleep on the plane.		
23 You should be more careful than usual of what and when you eat on the plane.		
24 It takes anything up to seven days to get over jet lag.		
25 When you arrive you should always try to sleep.		

PAPER 5 INTERVIEW (15–20 minutes)

You will be asked to take part in a conversation with a group of other students or with your teacher. The conversation will be based on one particular topic area or theme, for example holidays, work, food.

Of course each interview will be different for each student or group of students, but a *typical* interview is described below.

★ At the start of the interview you will be asked to talk about one of the photographs among the Interview Exercises at the back of the book.

★ You will then be asked to discuss one of the passages at the back of the book. Your teacher may ask you to talk about its content, where you think it comes from, who the author or speaker is, whether you agree or disagree with it, and so on. You will *not* be asked to read the passage aloud, but you may quote parts of it to make your point.

★ You may then be asked to discuss for example an advertisement, a leaflet, extract from a newspaper etc. Your teacher will tell you which of the Interview Exercises to look at.

★ You may also be asked to take part in an activity with a group of other students or your teacher. Your teacher will tell you which section among the Interview Exercises you should look at.

Practice Test 5

PAPER 1 READING COMPREHENSION (1 hour)

Answer all questions. Indicate your choice of answer in every case **on the separate answer sheet** *already given out, which should show your name and examination index number. Follow carefully the instructions about how to record your answers. Give* **one answer only** *to each question. Marks will not be deducted for wrong answers: your total score on this test will be the number of correct answers you give.*

SECTION A

In this section you must choose the word or phrase which best completes each sentence. **On your answer sheet** *indicate the letter A, B, C or D against the number of each item 1 to 25 for the word or phrase you choose.*

1 A part-time job gives me the freedom to .... my own interests.
  A pursue   B chase   C seek   D catch

2 The tennis player couldn't .... the possibility of withdrawing from the championship because of injury.
  A come off   B pass over   C rule out   D do without

3 I bought this fridge because I had confidence in the .... name.
  A mark   B maker   C commodity   D brand

4 This new advertising campaign is not .... with our company policy.
  A consistent   B allied   C suited   D matched

5 He became a millionaire by .... of hard work and a considerable amount of luck.
  A process   B effect   C dint   D cause

6 The union advised its members to resume .... working.
  A regular   B ordinary   C normal   D usual

7 'You can .... me the details: I don't want to know all about your arguments with your boss.'
  A spare   B save   C deprive   D avoid

8   People who take on a second job inevitably .... themselves to greater
    stress.
    A offer   B subject   C field   D place

9   The building work must be finished by the end of the month .... of
    cost.
    A ignorant   B thoughtless   C uncaring   D regardless

10 Sarah's friends all had brothers and sisters but she was a(n) .... child.
    A singular   B individual   C single   D only

11 .... from being embarrassed by his mistake, the lecturer went on
    confidently with his talk.
    A Distant   B Far   C A long way   D Miles

12 The increased pay offer was accepted although it .... short of what the
    employees wanted.
    A fell   B arrived   C came   D ended

13 The competition he set up for young musicians is another .... of his
    life-long support for the arts.
    A exposition   B manifestation   C token   D exhibition

14 Recent surveys have focused .... on the nation's health.
    A views   B opinion   C ideas   D attention

15 The new regime determined to .... compulsory military service.
    A stop off   B end up   C phase out   D break off

16 The professor's later work .... with the migration of birds.
    A specialised   B centred   C dealt   D concentrated

17 There were a number of strong candidates for the post but Peter's
    experience .... the scales in his favour.
    A weighted   B tipped   C balanced   D overturned

18 The family was made homeless through no .... of its own.
    A culpability   B blame   C responsibility   D fault

19 Children can be difficult to teach because of their short attention ....
    A limit   B span   C duration   D time

20 Christine's face .... up when she heard the good news.
    A showed   B cleared   C warmed   D lit

21 Few people can do creative work unless they are in the right .... of
   mind.
   A frame   B trend   C attitude   D tendency

22 The environmental .... of these chemicals went unrecognised for many
   years.
   A impression   B impact   C power   D force

23 Sheila couldn't attend the meeting as the date .... with her holidays.
   A clashed   B struck   C opposed   D occurred

24 Rail travellers can expect to face further .... as services are cut.
   A disruption   B disturbance   C derangement   D derailment

25 The development company .... approval from the council for their
   plans for a new shopping centre.
   A begged   B sought   C pleaded   D searched

SECTION B

*In this section you will find after each of the passages a number of questions or
unfinished statements about the passage, each with four suggested answers or ways of
finishing. You must choose the one which you think fits best. **On your answer sheet,**
indicate the letter A, B, C or D against the number of each item 26–40 for the answer
you choose. Give **one answer only** to each question. Read each passage right through
before choosing your answers.*

FIRST PASSAGE

By the time Shalini was twenty-two, the drama group which had given a
direction to her energies for six years began to disperse. For several months
she hung around the house in an aimless way that worried her mother,
Premila, far more than her being out too many evenings had ever done.
Then suddenly she told her mother that she had decided to apply for a place
in a college after all. Premila wanted to ask Shalini's uncles how to go about
it; Shalini had already found out what she needed to know, and within six
months had secured a grant and a place in college.

   Premila rejoiced to see her once again full of energy and enthusiasm.
There was an added bonus – now that Shalini had her life planned out for
the next three years, the uncles gave up talking about marriage so
insistently. College, unlike being unemployed, was respectable. It was
unfortunate that Shalini had applied to do drama rather than book-keeping,
or computer programming. But at least it was Education, and there would

be something measurable to add to Shalini's future value as a wife when finally she completed the course.

'A degree they can boast about when they are finding me a husband,' said Shalini, and laughed. Premila was shocked. 'Well, it's true,' Shalini said. 'You know that's how they think about it.' And however distressed Premila felt that her daughter should speak in that way about her uncles, she judged it was wiser not to scold her any more. Shalini's angry passion for the truth was like her father's though of course he would never have allowed her to express it as she did. Premila loved this quality in her daughter, as she had loved it in him . . . She stroked Shalini's hair lightly, and changed the subject, hoping that time would teach her that it is sometimes better not to say things, even if they are true.

Some time during Shalini's first year in college, Premila began to notice a change in her. It was difficult to define. Shalini was at home as often as before – perhaps more than when her evenings had been full of rehearsals. She still told Premila about little things that had happened each day. She brought her new college friends home, and remained responsible and affectionate towards her brothers. Yet Premila felt that the closeness with her daughter which for ten years had been the most significant feature of her emotional life was not there to be drawn upon in quite the same way. Eventually she identified what was missing between them – Shalini appeared to have no passions to share with her mother.

26   When Shalini was twenty-two, Premila was worried because
    A her energy suddenly disappeared.
    B she lost her sense of purpose.
    C she stayed at home too much.
    D her attitude to her family changed.

27   Before she went to college, Shalini's uncles were concerned because she
    A had uncertain prospects.
    B showed no interest in marriage.
    C enjoyed having no work.
    D had no interest in studying useful subjects.

28   Why were Shalini's uncles pleased about her decision to attend college?
    A They thought drama was a respectable profession.
    B They could stop thinking about her future.
    C She was less likely to remain single.
    D It came as a great relief to her mother.

29   Premila wished that her daughter could be less
    A truthful.
    B passionate.
    C rebellious.
    D outspoken.

30 After Shalini had started college, Premila felt that her daughter was
    A more confident.
    B more independent.
    C less loving.
    D less communicative.

SECOND PASSAGE

The houses of famous writers have, to me, an ambiguous quality. First, they
are houses like anyone else's. If they had not been once lived in by famous
people, there would be no plaque on the wall, no visitors to roam round the
rooms. In some cases ordinary people are living there, hardly aware of
the past illustrious occupants. But, to me, a famous writer's house is
irresistible; I find sheer magic in the rooms, in the staircases, in the
gardens. The more ordinary the scene, in fact, the more I succumb to
sensation, wonder and awe.

Once I found myself in the house of a famous living poet without at
first realising it. It was in wartime England, in the summer of 1944. I was
travelling from my home in Edinburgh to my job in the Foreign Office, my
department of which was in a county outside London. In the train I sat next
to a girl who was also going back to her job. She was a mother's help, she
told me, in a professor's family. The train arrived with five hours' delay, too
late for me to cross London and make my connection to the country. My
new friend asked me to come and spend the night with her at the house
where she worked; her employers were away, she said.

It was a warm summer evening, still light enough to see the small,
tangled garden in front of the house. We entered a large room almost
entirely filled by a long worktable of plain wood, just such a table as I myself
always write on now. The place was generally unconventional. I thought, at
first, unnecessarily so. It looked like eccentricity for its own sake. One room
had nothing but a mattress-bed on the floor. There was a handsome
writing-desk and a marvellous library of books. It was a decidedly literary
collection. I began looking through the titles.

I found two of the books, and then more, inscribed by famous
novelists. Another was dedicated to a famous poet, and so was yet another.
I called upstairs to my friend, who was now having a bath. 'Is this the house
of a famous poet?' 'Yes,' she called out, 'he writes poetry.'

The famous poet was Louis MacNeice, whose work I loved and
admired tremendously. I was rather embarrassed when I found myself in
Louis MacNeice's house. I made my new friend assure me there was no
likelihood of his return that night. I saw the house with new eyes, the
functional rightness and nobility of all it held.

I ran outside to look at the house from the point of view of my new
knowledge. I had never met a real poet. I have always known that this
occasion vitally strengthened my resolve to become a writer.

31 How did the author come to spend the night at the poet's house?
   A She had arranged to stay there with a friend.
   B She thought it sounded an interesting place to visit.
   C She couldn't complete her journey without a rest.
   D She didn't have anywhere to stay in London.

32 When she found out that the house belonged to a famous poet,
   A she was taken by surprise.
   B she understood certain aspects of the house.
   C she was eager to meet him.
   D she wanted to leave.

33 How did the visit affect her later life?
   A It established her as a writer.
   B It changed her views on poetry.
   C It determined her career.
   D She decided to become a poet.

34 What, for the author, was exciting about the house she visited?
   A The writer's possessions were on display for the public.
   B The exterior of the house was unusual.
   C The writer's presence could be sensed from his possessions.
   D The house had been visited by so many famous people.

THIRD PASSAGE

My car's gear lever does more than dispense transmission ratios. It panders to me. It cajoles and beckons. It wears out its chrome heart to make my life easier. For – as its manufacturers are quick to claim – the company devotes hundreds of man-hours to testing and retesting each possible design and configuration to see which does the job best. Which shape fits most naturally into a human hand. Which covering is most pleasing. And which overall look makes your fingers tremble with anticipation.

This curious pursuit, reputedly espoused by and entrenched within all of today's major manufacturing firms, is called *ergonomics*, defined as 'the degree to which the system has been developed with the human user in mind'. Personally, I love the concept. I even like the sound of the word. I wish only that the results lived up to the hype.

Recently, for example, I purchased a rowing machine for home exercise. Within minutes of unwrapping my booty, I realised the unit I was so cautiously dissecting did not in any way match the colour picture on the box. The assembly instructions hinted darkly that putting the contraption together would be only slightly less complex than building a nuclear reactor. Perseverance paid off, however. After applying equal amounts of time and luck, I was finally able to make my rower, er, row. But the only cogent ergonomic thought that went into the design of this product was the shape of the cardboard container it was packed in. That's ergonomics in the real world.

Take videocassette recorders. VCRs are like snowflakes – no two are quite alike. While all are intended to do more or less the same things – play, record now, record later – the actual designs are about as consistent and predictable as a roulette wheel. If you lose or misplace the manual, you end up with little more than a digital clock.

And then there is the ubiquitous microwave oven. What do those 'low', 'medium' and 'high' settings really hint at? Show me a consumer sufficiently schooled in the effect of microwave transmissions on food molecules to properly – and intuitively – select the optimal setting! Only small children, bless them, seem to know how to make these machines bend to their wills. 'Put it on high and blast it,' says my nine-year-old niece. I do. It works.

Can anyone truly say the modern car is designed with the human user in mind? Recall the last time you plopped behind the wheel of your neighbour's new vehicle. How quickly did you find the knob that popped open the bonnet or the hood? Were you able to adjust the left-side mirror without 'unadjusting' the right-side mirror, activating the headlight washers or wipers, or possibly lowering the convertible top? Did you know which lever to push or pull to slide the seat forward without simultaneously upsetting the angle of the seat back or exploding the pneumatically pressured back-support?

As with most of today's products, the only thing we really know about car seats is that, given the correct incentive, they *will* move. Beyond that, you – and your ergonomically inspired intuition – are completely on your own.

35 In the second paragraph, the writer suggests that research on ergonomics is
    A misdirected.
    B outdated.
    C ineffective.
    D uninteresting.

36 What does the incident with the rowing-machine indicate?
    A The machine was of poor quality.
    B There was too much packing.
    C The manufacturer's energies were misplaced.
    D The writer was not careful enough with the machine.

37 What disturbs the writer about video-recorders?
    A They are easily damaged.
    B They vary for no obvious reason.
    C It is difficult to operate them.
    D Buying one is a risk.

38   In the writer's opinion, what problem affects microwave ovens?
     A Children misuse them.
     B Some foods are better cooked by alternative methods.
     C They are still rather unpopular.
     D Most users do not understand how they work.

39   The controls of a modern car are criticised for being
     A difficult to identify.
     B less than reliable.
     C too sophisticated.
     D badly positioned.

40   How does the writer view the application of ergonomic principles?
     A It spoils the appearance of products.
     B It fails to make products easier to use.
     C It has a bad effect on the quality of the product.
     D It makes the product too expensive.

PAPER 2   COMPOSITION   (2 hours)

*Write **two only** of the following composition exercises. Your answers must follow exactly the instructions given. Write in pen, not pencil. You are allowed to make alterations, but make sure that your work is clear and easy to read.*

1   Describe either an amusing or an unfortunate incident which occurred during your school-days. (About 350 words)

2   In every large city in the world, public transport is of very great importance. Discuss why this is so and how it should be provided. (About 350 words)

3   Write a story entitled 'A Narrow Escape'. (About 350 words)

4   Your parents are on holiday abroad and you are living in their house to look after it. One night a severe storm causes considerable damage to the house. Write a letter to your parents telling them what has happened and what you are doing about it. Noted below are some examples of storm damage; use these to help you write the letter. (About 300 words)

   – roof and aerial damaged
   – broken windows
   – garage blocked by fallen tree
   – power failure
   – garden fence blown down

5   Basing your answer on your reading of the prescribed text concerned, answer **one** of the following. (About 350 words)

   ERNEST HEMINGWAY: *A Farewell to Arms*
   A critic once wrote: 'The ending is quite unforgettable in its sadness.' In your opinion what events during the course of the story led the critic to write this, and do you agree with him?

   OSCAR WILDE: *The Importance of Being Earnest*
   In the play, what is so important about being 'Earnest'?

   RUTH RENDELL: *A Judgement in Stone*
   Do you think the fate of the Coverdale family was inevitable, given Eunice Packman's childhood and family background?

PAPER 3 USE OF ENGLISH (2 hours)

SECTION A

1 *Fill each of the numbered blanks in the passage with* **one** *suitable word.*

With the coming of the motor car at the end of the last century a new era in personal transport was born. The early motorist certainly (1) .... his problems – perhaps the biggest one being (2) .... his vehicle would start or not. This problem has almost (3) .... today, but others have (4) .... its place. More traffic and faster vehicles mean that, (5) .... safe and reliable a car may be, its driver has to have (6) .... more driving skill than ever before.

Today's drivers cannot neglect their own direct and personal (7) .... for the accidents that happen on the road every year. A good driver has many things (8) .... his make-up. Some of (9) .... , such as experience and skill, will come only in (10) .... , but others – just as important – must (11) .... part of him from the start. These qualities are a (12) .... of responsibility for the safety of others, a determination to (13) .... on the job of driving, patience and courtesy. Together, these become what is generally known (14) .... the driver's 'attitude'.

(15) .... everyone is patient (16) .... nature or gifted with good (17) .... of concentration. But because attitude is (18) .... important a part of safe driving, every driver must (19) .... a real effort to develop these qualities – and this effort

must start from the (20) .... beginning of the first driving lesson.

2 *Finish each of the following sentences in such a way that it is as similar as possible in meaning to the sentence printed before it.*

EXAMPLE: I expect that he will get there by lunchtime.

ANSWER: I expect him *to get there by lunchtime.*

a) No-one has challenged his authority before.

This is the first time ....

b) 'If Brian doesn't train harder, I won't select him for the team,' said the manager.

The manager threatened ....

....

c) The hurricane blew the roof off the house.

The house ....

....

d) You'll certainly meet lots of people in your new job.

You are ....

....

e) I left without saying goodbye as I didn't want to disturb the meeting.

Rather ....

....

f) There aren't many other books which explain this problem so well.

In few other books ....

g) I dislike it when people criticise me unfairly.

I object ....

h) Robert is sorry now that he didn't accept the job.

Robert now wishes ....

3 *Fill each of the blanks with a suitable word or phrase.*

   EXAMPLE: He doesn't mind one way or the other; it makes *no difference to* him.

   a) 'You just stepped on my foot! Why .... where you are going?'

   b) All the restaurants were closed so it was .... well we had taken a packed lunch with us.

   c) The thief was believed .... the building through the upstairs window.

   d) Despite several warnings, the swimmers didn't .... of the danger-flag flying on the beach.

   e) Mark Spitz is the only person ever .... seven gold medals at the Olympic Games.

   f) I was surprised at .... so many people on the train.

4 *For each of the sentences below, write a new sentence* **as similar as possible in meaning to the original sentence** *but using the word given. This word* **must not be altered in any way**.

   EXAMPLE: Not many people attended the meeting.
             turnout

   ANSWER: *There was a poor turnout for the meeting.*

   a) If interest rates are cut, the economic situation may improve.
       reduction

       ....

       ....

   b) The architect's new design was heavily criticised.
       criticism

       ....

       ....

   c) Very little money was raised by the charity appeal.
       response

       ....

       ....

d) Ours is the only company allowed to import these chemicals.
monopoly

....

....

e) The coach's tactics were directly responsible for the team's defeat.
consequence

....

....

f) We have no idea where he is.
whereabouts

....

....

g) The policeman acted quickly and averted an accident.
prompt

....

....

h) This new record is certain to sell a lot of copies.
doubt

....

....

SECTION B

5 *Read the following passage, then answer the questions which follow it.*

Anyone for a Holiday?

In my experience of holidays, the most lushly written brochures produce
the most disappointing results. This is because of what you might call
the *counterlife* theory of holidays, which holds that what you might get
out of the experience will be the opposite of what you were promised, or
expected, or desired.   5
    You book into a four-star hotel, for instance. The five-star hotel next
door looks rather better, but you can't afford it or are not going to get
into this ostentatious game of stars. The hotel is constructed according to

'the most advanced building techniques'. This, it turns out, takes the form of a pioneering soundproofing technique which enables you to hear every sound from the next room more clearly than if it were made in your own. You lie awake listening to the sound of someone else's rhino-snores. Sleepless for three nights, you ask for a change of room. They can offer you only one other room: it is directly below the dance-floor, where, tonight, 'for your especial entertainment', an international clog-dancing competition is being held.

Next year you try camping instead. These days your tent is already erected. It is three feet away from the next tent, and that tent has a very loud portable colour television in it . . .

Alternatively, you could save yourself for a winter holiday, trusting that it will be nothing like the last one, when you gritted your teeth and went to the Canaries, only to experience the wettest February the locals could remember, while, back at home, it was the mildest February for 300 years.

However, as July approaches, it's hard to resist the siren clichés: that you need a break, that travel broadens the mind, that all work and no play . . .

Certainly most people do need a holiday by the time they take one. But this is often due, not to their hard work over an extended period, but the frantic activity of the last days before leaving – all that catching up with things you meant to do months ago: all the sorting out of tickets, passports, insurance, currency, all the queuing for trains, boats, planes. Small wonder that most people sleep out the first few days of their holidays. Or fall ill.

That travel broadens the mind may also be true, but nowadays most people travel quickly in order to sit tight and stay put. Only hitch-hiking students seem interested in the leisurely tour. For the rest of us it's a matter of exchanging one set of rooms for another (usually worse) set. People talk of holidays as an escape, but one thing you can never escape from is yourself.

As for the idea of coming back refreshed, this feeling usually fades as quickly as a tan, sometimes even faster. But perhaps the most crucial argument of all against holidays is this: however disastrous they can be, the chances are you will end up hopelessly addicted to the country you've visited. You'll then be correspondingly depressed to be back in your own country.

Someone even less keen on holidays than I am suggested that what we need is a simulation machine which will give us the illusion of having travelled abroad with none of the accompanying disappointment. Another, more draconian measure would be to introduce compulsory holidays in a part of the world that one hasn't been to before. But please, none of those eight-week holidays some people take. I'm only going if I can come back the same day.

a) Briefly explain what the writer means by the *'counterlife'* theory of holidays. (line 3)

....

....

b) What is meant by 'this ostentatious game of stars'? (line 8)

....

....

c) What example is given of a claim from a holiday brochure? How is this claim shown to be exaggerated?

....

....

....

d) Why are the words 'for your especial entertainment' enclosed in quotation marks? (line 15)

....

....

e) Why does camping turn out to be no better than staying in a hotel?

....

....

f) How does the writer's reference to a winter holiday illustrate his *counterlife* theory?

....

....

g) What phrase in the passage suggests a reluctance to go on a winter holiday?

....

h) In your own words, explain why the writer refers to the common reasons for going on a holiday as 'siren clichés'. (line 25)

....

....

i) What two reasons does the writer give for holidaymakers sleeping out the first days of a holiday?

....

....

j) According to the writer, why might travel not broaden the minds of most holidaymakers?

....

....

k) In your own words, explain the writer's 'most crucial argument' against foreign holidays. (lines 42–43)

....

....

l) In a paragraph of 70–90 words, summarise the writer's arguments against taking a holiday.

....

....

....

....

....

....

....

....

....

....

....

....

....

....

....

PAPER 4   LISTENING COMPREHENSION
(about 30 minutes)

PART ONE

You will hear a conversation between a bank manager and one of the bank's customers, Mrs Hodges, who wants to borrow some money. For questions 1–10 complete the form which the manager uses with a word or a short phrase, or by ticking the correct alternative.

Southern National Bank plc   *Commercial Loan Assessment Form*

Name : ......*Mrs Hodges*...

Nature of business : (1) ....

(2) Status of borrower (please tick (✓) box) :

Freelance ☐   Partner ☐

Sole proprietor ☐   Managing Director ☐

Years with Southern National :

as private customer : (3) ....

as commercial customer : (4) ....

Please list reasons why you require a loan :

(5) ....

(6) ....

(7) ....

....

Sum required : (8) ....

Does the customer demonstrate :

(9) knowledge of the market   yes/no

(10) clear financial planning   yes/no

PART TWO

Listen to the following telephone conversation between the sports editor of a newspaper and one of his photographers. They are discussing photographs taken at a motor race. For question 11, indicate the correct answer by ticking the appropriate letter, A, B, C or D. For questions 12–19, show which of the pictures the editor chooses by circling YES for the one he chooses and NO for the ones which he does not choose.

11   From the conversation it seems that

A the editor expected the photographer to deliver the film.

B the journalist admitted that he had made a mistake.

C the editor was prepared to accept the photographer's explanation.

D the photographer was expecting the editor to have the film.

A	
B	
C	
D	

12
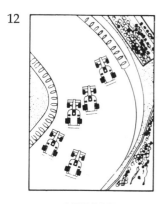
YES/NO

13

YES/NO

14
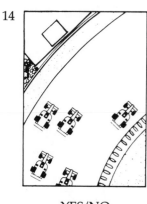
YES/NO

15
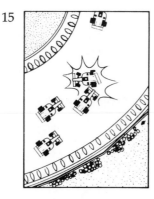
YES/NO

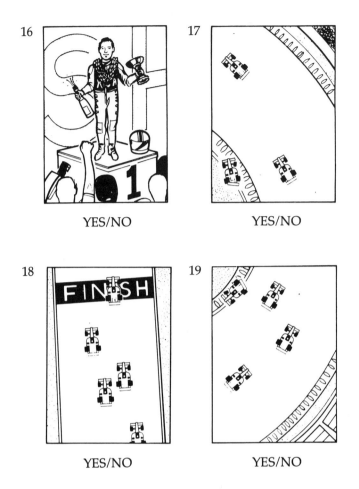

16   YES/NO

17   YES/NO

18   YES/NO

19   YES/NO

PART THREE

*You will hear a conversation between a married couple, Keith and Jane. The conversation begins as Keith is opening a letter. For questions **20–24** indicate the correct answer by putting a tick in the box next to the appropriate letter.*

20   How does Keith feel after reading the letter?

    A confused

    B indignant

    C resentful

    D incredulous

A	
B	
C	
D	

21   The magazine will not pay Keith because

    A he is not an established writer.

    B no British magazines pay reviewers.

    C it is Keith's first work for them.

    D plenty of people will do it for nothing.

A	
B	
C	
D	

22   Keith thinks the magazine succeeds because it

    A relies on its contributors' goodwill.

    B uses good writers.

    C saves money on writers' fees.

    D reaches a large number of readers.

A	
B	
C	
D	

23   Jane thinks Keith's first letter might

    A get the magazine to pay him.

    B make the magazine withdraw their offer.

    C cause trouble for him in the future.

    D make the magazine refuse to review his books.

A	
B	
C	
D	

24   Keith agrees to write a less angry letter because

    A he wants to avoid trouble later.

    B he does not want to be rude.

    C Jane insists on it.

    D he is short of money.

A	
B	
C	
D	

PAPER 5   INTERVIEW   (15–20 minutes)

You will be asked to take part in a conversation with a group of other students or with your teacher. The conversation will be based on one particular topic area or theme, for example holidays, work, food.

Of course each interview will be different for each student or group of students, but a *typical* interview is described below.

★ At the start of the interview you will be asked to talk about one of the photographs among the Interview Exercises at the back of the book.

★ You will then be asked to discuss one of the passages at the back of the book. Your teacher may ask you to talk about its content, where you think it comes from, who the author or speaker is, whether you agree or disagree with it, and so on. You will *not* be asked to read the passage aloud, but you may quote parts of it to make your point.

★ You may then be asked to discuss for example an advertisement, a leaflet, extract from a newspaper etc. Your teacher will tell you which of the Interview Exercises to look at.

★ You may also be asked to take part in an activity with a group of other students or your teacher. Your teacher will tell you which section among the Interview Exercises you should look at.

Interview Exercises

PRACTICE TEST 1

COMMUNICATING

1

2

3

4 In the revision, account has been taken of shifts in ideas and attitudes. Certain pejorative expressions and 'sexist language' have been removed and an enormous number of new expressions generated by the changes of the last twenty years added – Eurocrat, troubleshooter, credit cards, solar panels, boutique, multinationals, positive discrimination – to name but a few. The original edition of 1852 has sold more than 20 million copies.

5 I was walking with friends in the country when suddenly I felt this terrible pain in my side. I couldn't move and could hardly breathe. The pain was excruciating. It must have lasted almost a minute though it seemed longer. Then it passed and I waited for it to return but it didn't.
Later that day I learned that Jackie, my twin sister, had been involved in a car accident in London, a hundred miles away. The time of the accident was exactly the same as the time of my pain.

6 **Fax Machines**

The quickest, cheapest way to send documents . . .

A fax machine will transform your business by letting you send documents in a matter of seconds. An A4 page of text, graphics or plans can even be sent to the other side of the world in around a minute. Compare that to postal or courier delivery times!
Fax costs a fraction of a courier's charge and is cheaper than first-class post for a single A4 sheet sent within the UK.
Fax is easy to use, too. Just plug it into a standard telephone socket and power supply, and start faxing!

7 Technological advances in communications have made it increasingly possible to work away from the base. They have revolutionised, and will continue to revolutionise, not only the way we work but the way we live as well.

8 'If you are caught speaking your mother tongue, you will be punished.'

9 *Ways of communicating*

looks	body language	smoke
drums	smell	mirrors
flags	radar	touch
dreams		

PRACTICE TEST 2

THE ARTS

1

2

3

4 Newspapers are increasingly aware of the power of the still picture. The myth that paint depends on words – with pictures in a secondary role, employed, as old-timers say, 'to lighten the page' – persisted for a long time, but is now beginning to change. The photograph tells more than any words, as the following pages demonstrate.

5 Claude Monet's name is synonymous with Impressionism, yet his interpretation of the Impressionist style and technique was to change during the course of his long and prolific career. During the 1870s, like his fellow Impressionists Renoir, Sisley and Pissarro, he recorded suburban, urban and rural scenes under the fleeting effects of changing light, painting in short, comma-like brushstrokes with a brilliant and varied palette.

6 Listening to the Missa Solemnis, I wondered again why the work which Beethoven thought his greatest still has a forbidding image even among his legion admirers. Joseph Kerman, in his notes for the recording, calls it 'respected rather than loved'. Given Beethoven's undiminished power over music-lovers, and the prodigious impact and emotional intensity of the Mass, how can this be? Why does a work which bears the superscription 'From the heart – may it go to the heart' leave so many untouched?

7

a baby   a pet
someone you love a garden
a landscape   a house

8

Friday 21st – Saturday 22 Sept.
COMMUNITY ARTS CENTRE
NOBODIES FOOL

A clowning extravaganza, a
feast of folly you must not miss!
A brand new play that tumbles
through history, from Ship of
Fools to custard pie fights.

PRACTICE TEST 3

HISTORY

1

2

3

4

Gifts from Britain's Historic Heritage

If you share an interest in our island heritage, don't miss a visit to the Past Times shop. There you'll find a unique collection of authentic replicas, crafts and cards covering 4,000 years of Britain's History. From magnificent Roman jewellery and Medieval music tapes to Tudor pewter, elegant 18th Century prints and stunning Victorian design silk scarves ... pleasing and practical things from every age of Britain's past which you can buy and enjoy in your own home or choose as thoughtful presents for family and friends. Prices start at 35p, with many under £5.

5

The Heraklion Museum is the second largest Greek museum but unique in importance since, as the central museum of Crete, it represents almost exclusively the Minoan civilisation, the oldest civilisation developed on European soil. The movable remains of this great civilisation which extends over almost the whole of the third and second millennia BC are exhibited in chronological order throughout the twenty rooms and galleries of the museum.

6

In History's mysteries vast,
    The present's as strange as the past,
But before you condemn
I pray you, remem-
    ber, that you too are one of the cast.

7

8.00 pm – 9.00 pm
History Around the World
Another programme in this fascinating historical series showing events that have changed the course of history in countries all around the world. Tonight's programme features
................................?

8

What objects would you choose to bury for 200 years to represent the present age to later generations? Give reasons for your choices.

9   *History lessons*

   1 learning dates and facts
   2 reading history textbooks
   3 visiting museums and historical sites
   4 reading literature of the period
   5 looking at original documents
   6 watching a television programme or film

PRACTICE TEST 4

SUCCESS

1

2

3

4 Not only was he a remarkable man and a great leader of his people, but he also inspired a whole generation with his philosophy of non-violent resistance. His influence can be seen around the world and his life is an example of what simplicity, concern, common sense and dedication can do to change people's lives.

5

> Monica Seles of Yugoslavia won the Australian Open women's singles in Melbourne by defeating Jana Novotna of Czechoslovakia in the final, 5-7 6-3 6-1.
> Seles, who is 17, is in only her second year as a professional. In winning her second Grand Slam singles title, and beating by 4 months Margaret Court's record as the youngest winner of the Australian title, she passed $2m in career earnings, the 11th player to do so.

6 Arnold Schwarzenegger is a questionable actor but a huge star. James Caan is an excellent actor whom stardom has eluded. Schwarzenegger deliberately set out to promote his career, doing the rounds of the media parties and giving 100 interviews a day. Caan hated the Hollywood promotion and tried to keep himself out of the newspapers. While Schwarzenegger is a millionaire, Caan went broke and made no films for five years.

7 'If I hadn't become a millionaire by the age of 25, I would have considered myself a failure.'

'I put my work before my family but who knows if I was right or not? I've had a brilliant career and materially I want for nothing. My ex-husband has custody of our two children and I see them whenever I can.'

'I can no longer enjoy the simple things in life like going shopping.'

8
Einstein	Walt Disney
Madonna	Gorbachev
Picasso	Mozart
Napoleon	Mother Teresa
Henry Ford	Boris Becker

9 *'What is success?'*

career	manual skills
personal relationships	creativity
education	money
fame	luck

PRACTICE TEST 5

SOLITUDE OR COMPANY

1

2

3

4 If a situation becomes too crowded, then we adjust our reactions accordingly and allow our personal space to shrink. Jammed into an elevator, a rush-hour compartment, or a packed room, we give up altogether and allow body-to-body contact but adopt special techniques. We convert these other bodies into 'non-persons'. We studiously ignore them and they us. We try not to face them. We wipe all expressiveness from our faces, letting them go blank. Packed together like sardines in a tin, we stand dumbly still, sending out as few social signals as possible.

5 When from our better selves we have too long
Been parted by the hurrying world, and droop,
Sick of its business and of its pleasure tired,
How gracious, how benign is solitude.

6 In 4000 BC it is estimated that the total population was no more than 100 million. By the birth of Christ this had certainly doubled, but not until about 1800 did the number of people on earth exceed 1,000 million. Two thousand million was reached about 1930; 3,000 million in 1960; and 4,000 million in 1975. Today's population is about 4,600 million. With present rates of growth, by the year 2000 the earth will struggle to support close to 6,500 million people.

7 To control the escalating increase in world population we must have strong laws to limit the size of families. One child per couple should be the rule.

8

'Would you be able to survive alone on a desert island?'

(Shelter, food, loneliness, boredom, isolation, escape, etc.)

9

being an only child	or	a member of a large family
studying with a private teacher	or	in a large class
playing a solo instrument	or	as a member of an orchestra
being in hospital in a private room	or	in a large public ward
being a hostage in isolation	or	in a crowded prison
playing an individual sport	or	a team game
going on holiday alone	or	as a member of a large group

OPTIONAL READING

Ernest Hemingway: *A Farewell to Arms*

1

2

SEMPRE AVANTI !!

3

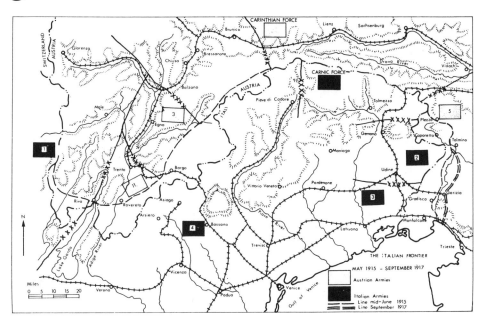

4

'Have you done nursing long?'

'Since the end of 'fifteen. I started when he did. I remember having a silly idea he might come to the hospital where I was. With a sabre cut, I suppose, and a bandage around his head. Or shot through the shoulder. Something picturesque.'

'This is the picturesque front,' I said.

5

'Open the bottle. Bring a glass. Drink that, baby. How is your poor head? I looked at your papers. You haven't any fracture. That major at the first post was a hog-butcher. I would take you and never hurt you. I never hurt anybody. I learn how to do it. Every day I learn to do things smoother and better. You must forgive me for talking so much, baby. I am very moved to see you badly wounded. There, drink that. It's good. It cost fifteen lire. It ought to be good. Five stars. After I leave here I'll go see that English and he'll get you an English medal.'

6 She went out. God knows I had not wanted to fall in love with her. I had not wanted to fall in love with anyone. But God knows I had and I lay on the bed in the room of the hospital in Milan and all sorts of things went through my head and finally Miss Gage came in. 'The doctor's coming,' she said. 'He telephoned from Lake Como.'

7 We backed a horse named Light for Me that finished fourth in a field of five. We leaned on the fence and watched the horses go by, their hoofs thudding as they went past, and saw the mountains off in the distance and Milan beyond the trees and the fields.

8 'Where will we live after the war?'
'In an old people's home probably,' she said. 'For three years I looked forward very childishly to the war ending at Christmas. But now I look forward till when our son will be a lieutenant-commander.'
'Maybe he'll be a general.'

9 'Halt,' I said. They kept on down the muddy road, the hedge on either side. 'I order you to halt,' I called. They went a little faster. I opened up my holster, took the pistol, aimed at the one who had talked the most, and fired. I missed and they both started to run. I shot three times and dropped one. The other went through the hedge and was out of sight. I fired at him through the hedge as he ran across the field. The pistol clicked empty and I put in another clip.

10 I looked at the carabinieri. They were looking at the newcomers. The others were looking at the colonel. I ducked down, pushed between two men, and ran for the river, my head down. I tripped at the edge and went in with a splash. The water was very cold and I stayed under as long as I could.

11 He bent down and shoved us off. I dug at the water with the oars, then waved one hand. The barman waved back deprecatingly. I saw the lights of the hotel and rowed out, rowing straight out until they were out of sight. There was quite a sea running but we were going with the wind.

12 It was fine country and every time that we went out it was fun. 'You have a splendid beard now,' Catherine said. 'It looks just like the woodcutters'. Did you see the man with the tiny gold earrings?' 'He's a chamois hunter,' I said. 'They wear them because they say it makes them hear better.'

13 I sat down on the chair in front of a table where there were nurses' reports hung on clips at the side and looked out of the window. I could see nothing but the dark and the rain falling across the light from the window. So that was it.

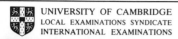

UNIVERSITY OF CAMBRIDGE
LOCAL EXAMINATIONS SYNDICATE
INTERNATIONAL EXAMINATIONS

ENGLISH AS A FOREIGN LANGUAGE

ENTER CANDIDATE
NUMBER HERE →

NOW SHOW THE
NUMBER BY
MARKING THE GRID

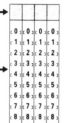

Examination/Paper No.

Examination Title

Centre No.

ENTER CANDIDATE NAME HERE:

....

- Tell the Invigilator immediately if the
information above is not correct.

MULTIPLE−CHOICE ANSWER SHEET

HOW TO ANSWER

Like this:

A   B   C   D   E

NOT like this:

A   B   C   D   E

A   B   C   D   E

A   B   C   D   E

HOW TO CHANGE YOUR ANSWER

Like this:

A   B

NOT like this:

A   B   C   D   E

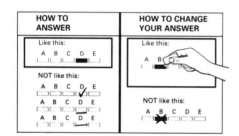

DO

– use an HB pencil
– rub out any answer
you wish to change

DON'T

– use any other kind of pen
or pencil
– use correcting fluid
– make any marks outside
the boxes

1	A B C D
2	A B C D
3	A B C D
4	A B C D
5	A B C D
6	A B C D
7	A B C D
8	A B C D
9	A B C D
10	A B C D

11	A B C D
12	A B C D
13	A B C D
14	A B C D
15	A B C D
16	A B C D
17	A B C D
18	A B C D
19	A B C D
20	A B C D

21	A B C D
22	A B C D
23	A B C D
24	A B C D
25	A B C D
26	A B C D
27	A B C D
28	A B C D
29	A B C D
30	A B C D

31	A B C D
32	A B C D
33	A B C D
34	A B C D
35	A B C D
36	A B C D
37	A B C D
38	A B C D
39	A B C D
40	A B C D

FCE/CPE-1 SUP   KENRICK■JEFFERSON   Printers to the Computer Industry   DP135/11

UNIVERSITY OF CAMBRIDGE
LOCAL EXAMINATIONS SYNDICATE
INTERNATIONAL EXAMINATIONS

ENGLISH AS A FOREIGN LANGUAGE

Examination/Paper No.

Examination Title

Centre/Candidate No.

Candidate Name

● Sign here if the information above is correct.

● Tell the Invigilator immediately if the
information above is not correct.

LISTENING COMPREHENSION ANSWER SHEET

ENTER ITEM
NUMBER HERE →

FOR OFFICE
USE ONLY → [10][20][30][40][50]
[1][2][3][4][5][6][7][8][9]

1	1	21	21
2	2	22	22
3	3	23	23
4	4	24	24
5	5	25	25
6	6	26	26
7	7	27	27
8	8	28	28
9	9	29	29
10	10	30	30
11	11	31	31
12	12	32	32
13	13	33	33
14	14	34	34
15	15	35	35
16	16	36	36
17	17	37	37
18	18	38	38
19	19	39	39
20	20	40	40